No God - No Peace

Know God - Know

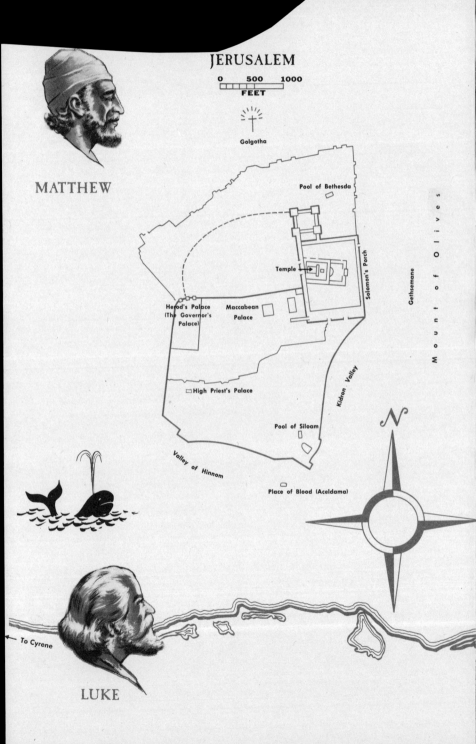

JERUSALEM

0   500   1000
FEET

Golgotha

MATTHEW

Pool of Bethesda

Temple

Solomon's Porch

Gethsemane

Mount of Olives

Herod's Palace
(The Governor's
Palace)

Maccabean
Palace

Kidron Valley

High Priest's Palace

Pool of Siloam

Valley of Hinnom

Place of Blood (Aceldama)

N

To Cyrene

LUKE

MARK

Abilene

Damascus

Sidon

Mount Hermon

Tyre

Philip's Caesarea

Iturea

Naphtali

Galilee

Chorazin
Capernaum
Bethsaida Julias
Bethsaida
Cana
Magdala
Plain of Gennesaret
Tiberias
LAKE OF GALILEE
Zebulun
Nazareth
Gadara
Nain

Ten Towns

Salim

Gerasa

Samaria

Sychar

Mount Gerizim

Arimathea

Ephraim

Jordan River

Perea

Emmaus
Rama
Jericho
Jerusalem
Bethphage
Bethany
Bethlehem
Bethany

Mediterranean Sea

Judea

Dead Sea

Machaerus

Kerioth

PALESTINE

0 5 10 15 20 25 30
SCALE OF MILES

Idumea

Sodom

JOHN

Phoenicia
Syria
Trachonitis

THE
CHRIST
OF THE
GOSPELS

THE
CHRIST
OF THE
GOSPELS

The life and work of
JESUS
as told by Matthew, Mark, Luke, and John

Presented as one complete story
in the language of today
by
William F. Beck

REVISED EDITION

CONCORDIA PUBLISHING HOUSE
St. Louis   London

Concordia Publishing House, St. Louis, Missouri
Concordia Publishing House Ltd., London, E. C. 1

© *1959 Concordia Publishing House*
© *1968, Revised Edition, Concordia Publishing House*

Library of Congress Catalog Card No. 59-11068

MANUFACTURED IN THE UNITED STATES OF AMERICA

Preface

If Jesus were talking to us today, He wouldn't use the strange words of long ago. He would talk to us in the language we use when we talk to one another. The purpose of this book is to let Jesus tell us His wonderful truths in our own language.

What He said and did was written down by Matthew, Mark, Luke, and John. And we have to read all four Gospels if we want the whole story of Jesus. Only Matthew and Luke tell us how Jesus was born. Only John tells us about the raising of Lazarus and the breakfast of the disciples with their risen Savior by the lake. Three of these writers, Matthew, Mark, and Luke, tell us about the Lord's Supper. But all four tell us how He suffered, died, and rose again.

How do the four Gospels fit together? How do the many events follow one another in the life of Christ? What was the one life of Jesus that all four writers tell us about? These are the problems which I have tried to solve. Here you will find everything in the four Gospels fitted together in one flowing story. Here is the life of Jesus from the time He came down to the earth until He returned to His Father.

It is a thrilling story, something never seen "on land or sea." It is the story of the Son of God, who loved us and gave Himself for us. Here we meet Him face to face, let Him talk to us, and as He goes to give His lifeblood for us, we let Him tell us, "Your sins are forgiven." And so He reaches with power into our lives, claims us as His own, never to let us go.

William F. Beck

The Life of Jesus

The Good News

about

JESUS CHRIST

God's Son

Luke Says

Many have undertaken to plan and write a story of what has been done among us, just as we heard it from those who from the first became eyewitnesses and servants of the Word. For this reason I too decided to check everything carefully from the beginning and to write it down in the proper order for you, excellent Theophilus, so that you will be sure what you have heard is true.

·1·
Jesus as a Child

An Angel Comes to Zacharias

When Herod was king in the country of the Jews, there was a priest by the name of Zacharias. He belonged to the division of priests named after Abijah. His wife was a descendant of Aaron, and her name was Elizabeth. Both were righteous before God as they lived blamelessly according to all the rules and regulations of the Lord.

But they had no children, because Elizabeth was barren and both were old.

Once Zacharias was on duty with his division and serving as priest before God. According to the custom of the priests he was chosen by lot to go into the Lord's temple to burn incense. All the people were praying outside while he was burning incense.

Then he saw the Lord's angel standing at the right side of the altar of incense. Zacharias was startled to see him and was terrified.

"Don't be afraid, Zacharias," the angel told him. *"Your*

prayer has been heard.[1] * You and *your wife* Elizabeth *will have a son, and you must call him* [2] John. He will be your joy and delight, and many will be glad he was born.

"He will be a great man before the Lord. *He will drink no wine or liquor.*[3] He will be filled with the Holy Spirit even before he is born. And he will bring many in Israel back to the Lord their God. He will go ahead of Him with the spirit and power of *Elijah, to move fathers to love their children,*[4] and the disobedient to think as righteous men — and so to get a people thoroughly prepared for the Lord."

"How can I be sure of this?" Zacharias asked the angel. "I'm an old man, and my wife is old."

"I am Gabriel!" the angel answered him. "I stand before God and was sent to speak to you and tell you this good news. And now, you will be silent and not able to talk till the day this happens, because you didn't believe what I said. But it will come true at the right time."

Meanwhile the people were waiting for Zacharias and were surprised he was staying so long in the holy place. When he did come out, he couldn't speak to them. Then they realized he had seen a vision in the holy place. He kept motioning to them and wasn't able to talk.

When the days of his service were over, he went home. After this, his wife Elizabeth conceived, and for five months she didn't show herself in public. "The Lord did this for me," she said. "I was feeling ashamed among people, but He was kind and helped me, and I don't have to feel ashamed anymore."

The Angel Comes to Mary

Five months later God sent the angel Gabriel to a town in Galilee called Nazareth, to a virgin engaged to a man by the name of Joseph, a descendant of David. The virgin's name was Mary.

* Old Testament words and quotations are in italics. Their sources are listed by number on pages 221 and 222.

Coming into her home, the angel said, "Greetings, you blessed one. The Lord is with you."

Startled by what he said, she tried to figure out what such a greeting might mean.

"Don't be afraid, Mary," the angel told her. "God is good to you. *You see, you will conceive and have a son, and you will call Him*[5] Jesus. He will be great and will be called *the Son of* the most high *God.* And the Lord will give Him *the throne of* His ancestor *David. He will be King over* the people of Jacob *forever, and His kingdom will never end.*"[6]

"How can this be?" Mary asked the angel. "I'm not living with a husband."

"The Holy Spirit will come over you," the angel answered her, "and a power of the most high God will overshadow you. And for that reason the Child will be called holy and God's Son. Now there is also Elizabeth, your relative. She is old, but she too conceived. People call her childless, but she's now in her sixth month. *There's nothing that God will not be able to do.*"[7]

"I am the Lord's servant," Mary answered. "Let it happen to me as you said."

Then the angel left her.

Mary Visits Elizabeth

Then Mary hurried away to the hill country to a town of Judah. There she went into the home of Zacharias and greeted Elizabeth.

When Elizabeth heard Mary's greeting, the baby leaped in her womb. Then Elizabeth was filled with the Holy Spirit, and she shouted, "Blessed are you among women, and blessed is the Child in your womb. But how does this happen to me that the mother of my Lord comes to me? The moment I heard your greeting, the baby leaped with delight in my womb. And you are happy for believing that the Lord will do what He promised you."

Mary said:

"*My soul* is praising *the Lord*,
And my spirit *delights in God, my Savior,*[8]
Because *He has looked kindly at His humble servant.*[9]
Yes, from now on the people in all the ages will call me
    blessed.
He has done great things to me —
    He who is mighty
    And *whose name is holy* [10]
    And *who is always merciful to those who fear Him.*[11]

"Mighty are the deeds He has done *with His arm.*
He has scattered [12] those who feel and think so proudly.
He has pushed strong rulers down from their thrones
    And *lifted up lowly people.* [13]
Those who were hungry He has filled with good things,[14]
And the rich He has sent away empty-handed.

"*He has come to help His servant Israel,*[15]
Because He wants to *remember His mercy* [16]
    (as *He promised our fathers*),
*The mercy He has for Abraham
    and his descendants forever.*" [17]

Mary stayed with Elizabeth about three months and then
went back home.

John Is Born

The time came for Elizabeth to give birth, and she had
a baby boy. Her neighbors and relatives heard how the
Lord had been unusually kind to her, and they were happy
with her.

On the eighth day they came to circumcise the baby.
They were going to call him Zacharias because that was his
father's name. But his mother spoke up. "No!" she said. "He's
going to be called John."

"But there's nobody among your relatives who has that name," they told her.

Then they motioned to his father to see what name he might want him to have. He asked for a writing tablet and wrote, "His name is John." They were all surprised.

Just then he got his speech back and could talk again. He began to speak, praising God.

All who lived around them were overawed. And all over the hills of Judea people kept talking about all these things. All who heard of them kept them in mind. "What is this child going to be?" they asked. It was clear — the Lord's hand was with him.

His father Zacharias was filled with the Holy Spirit, and he prophesied:

"Praise the Lord, the God of Israel,[18]
Because He has visited *His people*
    And prepared *a ransom for them.*[19]
He has *given* a descendant of His servant *David*
    To be our *victorious Savior,*[20]
As He said long ago through His holy prophets
That *He would save* us *from* our *enemies,*
    From the power of all *who hate* [21] us.
He wanted to be *merciful to our fathers* [22]
And *keep in mind His* holy *covenant,*
    The oath He swore to our father *Abraham*
To rescue us from our *enemies* [23]
And let us serve Him without fear
    In holiness and righteousness before Him all our life.

"And you, child, will be called a prophet of the most high
    God.
You will go *ahead of the Lord to prepare the ways for
    Him,*[24]
To tell His people they can be saved
    by the forgiveness of their sins,

Because our God is merciful
And will let a heavenly Sun rise among us,
*To shine on those who sit in the dark
and in the shadow of death* [25]
And to guide our feet into *the way of peace.*" [26]

An Angel Comes to Joseph

This is how Jesus Christ was born.

His mother Mary had promised Joseph to be his wife. But before they lived together, it was found that she was going to have a child — by the Holy Spirit. Joseph, her husband, was a good man and didn't want to disgrace her. So he decided to divorce her secretly.

After he thought about it, he in a dream saw the Lord's angel, who said, "Joseph, son of David, don't be afraid to take your wife Mary home with you; her Child is from the Holy Spirit. She will have a Son, and you will call Him Jesus, because He will save His people from their sins. All this happened so that what the Lord said through the prophet would come true: *The virgin will conceive and have a Son, and He will be called Immanuel,*" [27] which means God-with-us.

When Joseph awoke, he did what the Lord's angel had ordered him to do. He took his wife home with him but didn't live with her as a husband till she had a Son. And he called Him Jesus.

Jesus Is Born

In those days Emperor Augustus ordered a census taken of the whole world. This was the first census, and it was taken while Quirinius was ruling Syria. Everybody went to register, each to his own town.

Joseph also went up from the town of Nazareth in Galilee to David's town, called Bethlehem, in Judea, because he was one of the descendants of David, to register with Mary, his bride, who was going to have a child.

And while they were there, the time came for her to have her child. She had her first Son, and she wrapped Him up and laid Him in a manger because there was no room for them in the inn.

The Shepherds

There were shepherds not far away, living in the field and taking turns watching their flock during the night.

Then the Lord's angel stood by them, and the Lord's glory shone around them. They were terrified. "Don't be afraid," the angel said to them. "I have good news for you. A great joy will come to all the people: The Savior, who is Christ the Lord, was born for you today in David's town. And this is how you will know Him: you will find a Baby all wrapped up and lying in a manger."

Suddenly there was with the angel a large crowd of the angels of heaven, who were praising God and saying: "Glory to God in the highest heavens, and on earth peace among people who have His goodwill!"

When the angels had left them and gone to heaven, the shepherds said to one another, "The Lord has told us what has happened. Let's go to Bethlehem and see it."

They hurried over there and searched until they found Mary and Joseph, and the Baby lying in the manger. When they had seen Him, they told others what they had been told about this Child. And everybody was surprised to hear the story the shepherds told.

But Mary treasured all these things in her heart and kept thinking about them.

The shepherds went back, glorifying and praising God for everything they had heard and seen. It was just as they had been told.

In the Temple

On the eighth day the time came to circumcise the Child, and Joseph called Him Jesus, the name the angel gave Him before He was conceived.

When *the time came* for them *to be purified* [28] according to the Law of Moses, Joseph and Mary took Jesus up to Jerusalem to give Him to the Lord (as it is written in the Law of the Lord, *Every firstborn boy should be* called *the Lord's holy one* [29]) and to offer a sacrifice according to the Law of the Lord, *a pair of turtledoves or two young pigeons.* [30]

Now, there was in Jerusalem a man by the name of Simeon. He was a good man, fearing God and waiting for the One who would comfort Israel. The Holy Spirit was on him. The Holy Spirit had told him that before he would die he would see the Savior sent by the Lord.

Moved by the Spirit, he went into the temple. When the parents brought in the Child Jesus to do for Him what was customary according to the Law, Simeon took Him in his arms, praised God, and said:

"Lord, now You are letting Your servant go in peace as
    You promised,
Because my eyes have *seen Your salvation* [31]
That You prepared for all people to see,
A light to shine on the Gentiles,
And the *glory of* Your people *Israel.*" [32]

His father and mother were surprised such things were said about Him. Then Simeon blessed them and said to His mother Mary, "Here is what this Child is appointed for: Many in Israel will fall and rise again because of Him; and He'll be a sign that many will talk against, to show what they're thinking in their hearts. And pain, like a sword, will go through your own soul too."

Anna, a prophetess, was also there. She was a daughter of Phanuel, of the tribe of Asher. She was now very old. When she was a girl, she had married a man and lived with him seven years. After that she was a widow till she was eighty-four. She never left the temple but worshiped day and night, fasting and praying. She too came forward just then, thanked God, and talked about the Child to all who were looking for Jerusalem to be set free.

Joseph and Mary did everything the Law of the Lord told them to do.

The Wise Men

Jesus was born in Bethlehem in Judea when Herod was king. Then Wise Men came from the east to Jerusalem. "Where is the Child who was born King of the Jews?" they asked. "We saw His star rise and have come to worship Him."

When King Herod heard about this, he became alarmed and all Jerusalem with him. He called together all of the people's ruling priests and men trained in the Bible and tried to find out from them where the promised Savior was to be born.

"In Bethlehem, in Judea," they told him, "because the prophet has written: *And you, Bethlehem,* land of Judah, *are* not at all *the least among the leading towns of Judah, since from you will come a leader who will be the Shepherd of My people Israel."* [33]

Then Herod secretly called the Wise Men and found out from them the exact time the star appeared. Then he sent them to Bethlehem. "Go and search carefully for the little Child," he said. "And when you find Him, report to me, so that I too may go and bow down before Him."

After hearing the king, they started out. And there was the star they had seen when it rose! It led them on till it came to a stop over the place where the Child was. They were extremely happy to see the star. They went into the house and saw the little Child with His mother Mary. Kneeling, they worshiped Him. Then they opened their treasure chests and offered Him *gifts: gold, incense,* [34] and myrrh.

February, 4 B. C., and later   19

But God warned them in a dream not to go back to Herod. So they went home to their country by another road.

To Egypt!

After the Wise Men left, Joseph in a dream saw the Lord's angel, who said, "Get up, take the little Child and His mother, and flee to Egypt. Stay there till I tell you. Herod is going to search for the Child to kill Him."

Joseph got up at night, took the little Child and His mother, and went to Egypt. He stayed there till Herod died. In this way what the Lord said through the prophet was to come true: *I called My Son from Egypt.*[35]

When Herod saw that the Wise Men had tricked him, he got very angry and sent men to kill all the boys in Bethlehem and in all the country around it, up to two years old, according to the exact time he had found out from the Wise Men. Then what the prophet Jeremiah said came true:

> *A cry is heard in Rama!*
> *Weeping and bitter wailing:*
> *Rachel crying over her children*
> *And refusing to be comforted*
> *Because they are gone.*[36]

But when Herod died, the Lord's angel appeared to Joseph in Egypt in a dream and told him, "Get up, take the little Child and His mother, and go to the land of Israel. Those who tried to kill the little Child are dead."

Joseph got up, took the little Child and His mother, and came to the land of Israel. But when he heard, "Archelaus has succeeded his father Herod as king of Judea," he was afraid to go back there. And being warned in a dream, they went back to Galilee to their town of Nazareth. There Joseph made his home. And so what the prophets said came true: Jesus was to be called a man from Nazareth.*

* According to Is. 11:1 the Savior would be a Nezer, a sprout, growing from the roots of the tree of David.

The Boy Jesus

The little Child grew big and strong and full of wisdom, and God's love was with Him.

Every year His parents would go to Jerusalem to celebrate the Passover. And so when He was twelve, they went up for the festival as usual.

When the festival days were over and they started for home, the boy Jesus stayed behind in Jerusalem. But His parents didn't know about it. They thought He was with the others who were traveling with them. After traveling a day, they started to look for Him among their relatives and friends. When they didn't find Him, they went back to Jerusalem looking for Him.

Two days later they found Him in the temple, sitting among the teachers, listening to them and asking them questions. His understanding and His answers surprised all who heard Him.

His parents were amazed to see Him there. "Son, why did You do this to us?" His mother asked Him. "See how anxiously Your father and I have been looking for You!"

"Why were you looking for Me?" He asked them. "Didn't you know I must be in My Father's house?" But they didn't understand what He told them.

Then He went back with them to Nazareth. And He obeyed them.

His mother kept all these things in her heart. And Jesus grew wiser and taller and *won the approval of God and of people.*[37]

· 2 ·

John and Jesus

John Prepares the Way

The child John grew and became strong in spirit. He lived in the wilderness till he appeared publicly before Israel. In the fifteenth year of the rule of Emperor Tiberius, Pontius Pilate was governor of Judea, Herod ruled Galilee, his brother Philip ruled Iturea and Trachonitis, Lysanias ruled Abilene, and Annas and Caiaphas were the high priests. Then God spoke to John, the son of Zacharias, in the wilderness.

John the Baptizer was dressed in camel's hair with a leather belt around his waist. And he lived on grasshoppers and wild honey.

He appeared in the wilderness of Judea and preached: "Repent — the kingdom of heaven is near." He went into the whole Jordan valley and preached: "Repent and be baptized to have your sins forgiven."

He was the one of whom the prophet Isaiah had said in

his book: *I will send My messenger ahead of You to prepare the way* [38] *for You.*

Someone will be calling in the wilderness:
"Prepare the way for the Lord,
Make the paths straight for Him.
Every ravine must be filled,
And every mountain and hill must be cut down.
The crooked must be made straight
And the rough roads smooth.
All people must see how God saves them." [39]

Then all the people of Jerusalem, all Judea, and the whole Jordan valley came out to him. As they confessed their sins, he baptized them in the Jordan River.

Among the crowds who were coming out to be baptized by him he also saw many Pharisees and Sadducees coming for baptism. "Brood of snakes, who warned you to run away from the punishment waiting for you?" he asked them. "Do the works that show you have repented. And don't start telling yourselves, 'Abraham is our father.' I tell you, God can raise children for Abraham from these stones. The ax is now ready to strike at the roots of the trees, and any tree that doesn't produce good fruit will be cut down and thrown into the fire."

"What should we do?" the crowds asked him.

"If you have two garments," he answered them, "share them with him who has none, and if you have food, do the same."

Some tax collectors also came to be baptized. "Teacher," they asked him, "what should we do?"

"Don't collect more money than you're ordered to collect," he told them.

Some soldiers also asked him, "And what should we do?"

"Don't use threats or blackmail to get money from anyone," he told them, "but be satisfied with your pay."

The people were expecting something, and all were wondering if John was perhaps the promised Savior. John answered them all and preached: "I baptize you with water for a change of heart. But the One who is coming after me is mightier than I. I'm not good enough to bend down and untie His shoe straps and carry away His shoes. He will baptize you with the Holy Spirit and fire. He has the winnowing shovel in His hand and will clean up His threshing floor. His wheat He'll gather into His barn, but the chaff He'll burn in a fire that can't be put out."

And so with many other challenging words he was telling the people the good news.

John Baptizes Jesus

It was in those days, when all the people were being baptized, that Jesus came from Nazareth in Galilee to John at the Jordan to be baptized by him. John tried to stop Him. "I need to be baptized by You," he said, "and You come to me?"

"Let Me have My way now," Jesus answered him. "That is how we should accomplish every righteous purpose."

Then John gave in to Him and baptized Him in the Jordan. Just as He stepped out of the water, while He was praying, He saw heaven torn open and God's Holy Spirit coming down on Him in the bodily form of a dove. And a voice from heaven said, "You are *My Son,* whom I love. *I am delighted* [40] with You."

Jesus was about thirty years old when He began His work.

The Devil Tempts Jesus

Then Jesus, full of the Holy Spirit, left the Jordan. The Spirit drove Him out into the wilderness to be tempted by the devil. For forty days the Spirit led Him in the wilderness while the devil tempted Him. He was there with the wild animals. He didn't eat anything for forty days and then got hungry.

The devil, the tempter, came to Him and said, "If you're God's Son, tell these stones to become loaves of bread."

"It is written," Jesus answered him, "*A man doesn't live on bread alone but on every word that God speaks.*" [41]

Then the devil took Him into Jerusalem, the Holy City, and had Him stand on the edge of the temple. "If You're God's Son," he told Him, "jump down from here. It is written: *He will order His angels to watch carefully over you. They will carry you in their hands* and *never let you stub your foot against a stone.*" [42]

"It is also written," Jesus answered him, "*Don't test the Lord your God.*" [43]

Then the devil took Him up a very high mountain and in a moment showed Him all the kingdoms in the world and their glory. "I'll give You all this power and glory," the devil told Him, "because it was given to me and I give it to anyone I please. So, if You'll bow down and worship me, all this will be Yours."

Then Jesus answered him, "Go away, devil! It is written: Worship *the Lord your God, and serve Him* only." [44]

When the devil had finished every way of tempting Him, he left Him till the right time would come. And angels came and served Him.

The Word Became Flesh

In the beginning was the Word, and the Word was with God, and the Word was God. He was in the beginning with God.

Everything was made by Him, and not one thing that was made was made without Him.

In Him was life, and the Life was the Light of men. The Light is shining in the dark, and the darkness has not put it out.

A man came — God sent him — his name was John. He came to tell the truth about the Light to help everyone believe. He was not the Light but came to tell the truth about the Light.

The true Light that gives light to everyone was coming into the world. He was in the world, and He made the world, and the world didn't know Him. He came to His own, and His own people didn't welcome Him. But to all who welcomed Him, who believe in His name, He gave the power to become God's children. They have been born, not of the blood of parents or of a sexual desire or of a man's desire but of God.

And the Word became flesh and lived among us as in the tabernacle, and we saw His glory, a glory of the only Son from His Father, full of love and truth.

John told the truth about Him when he called: "This is the One of whom I said, He who is coming after me is ahead of me because He was before me."

All of us have taken from all that is in Him — gift after gift of His love. The Law was given through Moses, but Jesus Christ brought love and truth. Nobody has ever seen God. The only Son who is God and close to the Father's heart has told us about Him.

Lamb of God

When the Jews in Jerusalem sent priests and Levites to John to ask him, "Who are you?" this was John's testimony. He confessed and didn't deny. He confessed: "I'm not the promised Savior."

"What are you then?" they asked him. "Are you Elijah?"

"I am not," he said.

"Are you the Prophet?"

"No," he answered.

Then they asked him, "Who are you? We want to bring an answer to those who sent us. What do you say about yourself?"

He said:"I am *someone calling in the wilderness, 'Make straight the way for the Lord,'* [45] as the prophet Isaiah said."

Some who had been sent belonged to the Pharisees. They asked him, "Why, then, do you baptize if you're not the promised Savior or Elijah or the Prophet?"

"I baptize with water," John answered them. "There is standing among you Someone you don't know, the One who is coming after me. I'm not good enough to untie His shoe strap."

This happened at Bethany on the other side of the Jordan, where John was baptizing.

The next day John sees Jesus coming toward him. And he says, "Look at the Lamb of God who takes away the sin of the world. He is the One I meant when I said, 'A Man is coming after me but is ahead of me, because He was before me.' Even I didn't know who He was, but I came and baptized with water to show Him to Israel."

John testified: "I saw the Spirit come down from heaven as a dove and stay on Him. I didn't know who He was, but He who sent me to baptize with water told me, 'When you see the Spirit come down on Someone and stay on Him, He is the One who baptizes with the Holy Spirit.' I saw it and testified, 'This is the Son of God.'"

The First Disciples

The next day, while John was again standing with two of his disciples, he saw Jesus passing by. "Look at the Lamb of God!" he said. When the two disciples heard him say this, they followed Jesus.

Jesus turned around and saw them following. "What are you looking for?" He asked them.

"Rabbi" (which means Teacher), "where are You staying?" they asked Him.

"Come and you'll see," He told them. So they came and saw where He was staying, and they stayed with Him that day. It was about ten in the forenoon.

One of the two who heard John and then followed Jesus

was Andrew, Simon Peter's brother. He first found his own brother Simon and told him, "We have found the promised Savior." (The Greek word for Him is Christ.) He brought him to Jesus.

Looking at him, Jesus said, "You are Simon, John's son. Your name will be Cephas"* (which means Peter*).

The next day Jesus wanted to go to Galilee. He found Philip. "Follow Me!" Jesus told him. Philip was from Bethsaida, the hometown of Andrew and Peter.

Philip found Nathanael and told him, "The One Moses wrote about in the Law, and the prophets too — we've found Him, Jesus, Joseph's Son from Nazareth."

"Nazareth — can anything good come from there?" Nathanael asked him.

"Come and see!" Philip told him.

Jesus saw Nathanael coming toward Him. "Here's a real Israelite in whom there is no deceit," He said of him.

"Where did You get to know me?" Nathanael asked Him.

"Before Philip called you," Jesus answered him, "when you were under the fig tree, I saw you."

"Master," Nathanael answered Him, "You are God's Son! You are Israel's King!"

"You believe because I told you I saw you under the fig tree," Jesus answered him. "You will see greater things than that." And He said to him, "I tell you people the truth, you will see *heaven* opened *and God's angels going up and coming down* [46] on the Son of Man."

Jesus Changes Water to Wine

Two days later there was a wedding in Cana in Galilee, and Jesus' mother was there. Jesus and His disciples had also been invited to the wedding.

When the people were out of wine, Jesus' mother said to Him, "They don't have any wine."

* Cephas in Aramaic and Peter in Greek both mean "rock."

"Will you leave that to Me, woman?" Jesus asked her. "It isn't the right time yet."

His mother told the waiters, *"Do anything He tells you."* [47]

Six stone water jars were standing there for the religious washings of the Jews. Each jar held eighteen to twenty-seven gallons.

"Fill the jars with water," Jesus told them. And they filled them to the top. "Now take some of it," He told them, "and bring it to the manager of the dinner." So they brought it to him.

When the manager tasted the water that had been changed to wine, he didn't know where it was from; only the waiters who had dipped the water knew. So the manager called the groom. "Everybody serves his good wine first," he told him, "and when people have drunk much, then the poorer wine. You've kept the good wine till now."

Jesus did this, the first of His miracles, in Cana in Galilee. He showed His glory, and His disciples believed in Him.

After this He, His mother, His brothers, and His disciples went down to Capernaum and stayed there a few days.

Jesus Cleans the Temple

The Jewish Passover was near, so Jesus went up to Jerusalem.

In the temple He found men selling cattle, sheep, and pigeons, and the money changers were sitting there. So He made a whip of small ropes and with their sheep and cattle drove them all out of the temple. He scattered the coins of the money changers and upset their tables.

"Take these away!" He told those who sold pigeons. "Don't make My Father's house a place for business."

His disciples had to think of what the Bible said: *The zeal for Your house will consume Me.* [48]

Then the Jews came back at Him by asking, "By what miracle can You prove to us You may do this?"

"Tear down this temple," Jesus answered them, "and I will raise it in three days."

"It took forty-six years to build this temple," said the Jews, "and You'll raise it in three days?"

But the temple He spoke of was His own body. After He rose from the dead, His disciples remembered He had said this, and they believed the Bible and what Jesus had said.

Nicodemus

Now, while He was in the crowd at the Passover in Jerusalem, many believed in His name when they saw the miracles He was doing. Jesus, however, wouldn't trust them, because He knew everybody. He didn't need to be told about anyone, because He knew what was in him.

Now, there was a Pharisee by the name of Nicodemus, a member of the Jewish court. He came to Jesus one night. "Master," he said to Him, "we know You're a teacher who has come from God. Nobody can do these miracles You do unless God is with him."

"I tell you the truth," Jesus answered him, "if anyone isn't born from above, he can't see God's kingdom."

"How can anyone be born when he's old?" Nicodemus asked Him. "He can't go back into his mother's womb and be born again, can he?"

"I tell you the truth," Jesus answered him, "if anyone isn't born of water and the Spirit, he can't get into God's kingdom. Anything born of the flesh is flesh, but anything born of the Spirit is spirit. Don't be surprised when I tell you you must all be born from above. The wind blows where it pleases and you hear the sound of it, but you don't know where it's coming from or where it's going. So it is with everyone born of the Spirit."

"How can that be?" Nicodemus asked Him.

"You are the teacher in Israel," Jesus said to him, "and don't know this? I assure you, We tell what We know, and We testify to what We have seen. But you people don't accept Our testimony. If you don't believe the earthly things I told you, how will you believe Me if I tell you heavenly things? No one has gone up to heaven except the One who came down from heaven — the Son of Man.

"As Moses lifted up the snake in the desert, so the Son of Man must be lifted up so that everyone who believes in Him has everlasting life. God so loved the world that He gave His only Son so that everyone who believes in Him doesn't perish but has everlasting life. You see, God didn't send His Son into the world to condemn the world but to save the world through Him. If you believe in Him, you're not condemned. But if you don't believe, you're already condemned because you don't believe in the name of God's only Son. This is why people are condemned: The Light came into the world, but people have loved darkness instead of the Light because they have been doing wrong. Everyone who does wrong hates the Light and will not come to the Light — he doesn't want his works to be seen in the light. But anyone who lives in the truth comes to the Light so that his works may be seen to have been done in God."

John Is Happy in Jesus

After this, Jesus and His disciples went into the country of Judea, and there He spent some time with them and baptized.

John too was baptizing in Aenon, near Salim, because there was much water there. So people came and were baptized. John had not yet been put in prison.

John's disciples started a discussion with a Jew about religious cleansing, and they came to John. "Teacher," they told him, "He who was with you on the other side of the Jordan and to whom you gave your testimony — He's here. He's baptizing, and everybody's going to Him."

"A man can get only what Heaven has given him," John answered. "You yourselves are witnesses that I said I'm not the promised Savior but am sent ahead of Him.

"The One who has the bride is the Bridegroom. The Bridegroom's friend stands and listens to Him. And when the Bridegroom speaks, He makes His friend very happy. Now, this is my happiness, and it's complete. He must grow while I must become less. The One who comes from above is above all others.

"Anyone who comes from the earth is earthly and talks about earthly things. The One who comes from heaven is above all others. He tells the truth of what He has seen and heard, and nobody accepts the truth He tells. But anyone who has accepted the truth He tells has stamped with his seal of approval that God tells the truth. The One whom God has sent says what God says because God gives Him His Spirit without a limit. The Father loves the Son and has put everything in His hands. Anyone who believes in the Son has everlasting life. But anyone who will not listen to the Son will not see life, but God will always be angry with him."

John in Prison

John was showing Herod, the governor, how wrong he was in regard to his brother's wife Herodias and all the other wicked things Herod did. Herod had married Herodias, the wife of his brother Philip. "It isn't right for you to have your brother's wife," John told Herod. He, on top of everything, sent men who arrested John, bound him, and locked him up in prison.

The Lord found out that John had been put in prison and that the Pharisees had heard, "Jesus is making and baptizing more disciples than John," although it wasn't really Jesus but His disciples who baptized. Then He left Judea.

· 3 ·

First Tour of Galilee

The Samaritan Woman

Jesus started back on the way to Galilee, and He had to go through Samaria. He came to a town in Samaria by the name of Sychar, near the piece of land Jacob gave his son Joseph. Jacob's Well was there. So Jesus, tired as He was from traveling, sat down by the well. It was about six in the evening.

A woman of Samaria came to draw water. "Give Me a drink," Jesus said to her. His disciples had gone into the town to buy food.

The Samaritan woman asked Him: "How can You, a Jew, ask me, a Samaritan woman, for a drink?" Jews, you see, don't drink from the same jar with Samaritans.

"If you knew what God is giving," Jesus answered her, "and who it is that says to you, 'Give Me a drink,' you would have asked Him, and He would have given you living water."

Samaria, early summer, A. D. 27   35

"Sir, You have nothing to draw water with," she told Him, "and the well is deep. Where can You get living water from a spring? Are You greater than Jacob, our ancestor, who gave us the well? He himself drank from it, and also his sons and his animals."

"Everyone who drinks this water," Jesus answered her, "will get thirsty again. Anyone who drinks the water I'll give him will never get thirsty again. But the water I'll give him will be in him a spring of water bubbling up to everlasting life."

"Sir, give me this water," the woman told Him. "Then I won't get thirsty or have to come out here to draw water."

"Go, call your husband," Jesus told her, "and come back here."

"I don't have any husband," the woman answered Him.

"You're right when you say, 'I don't have any husband,'" Jesus told her. "You've had five husbands, and the man you have now isn't your husband. You've told the truth!"

"Sir," the woman said to Him, "I see You're a prophet! Our ancestors worshiped on this mountain, but you say, 'The place where people must worship is in Jerusalem.'"

"Believe Me, woman," Jesus told her, "the time is coming when you will not be worshiping the Father on this mountain or in Jerusalem. You don't know what you're worshiping. We know what we're worshiping, because salvation comes from the Jews. But the time is coming, and it is here now, when real worshipers will worship the Father in spirit and in truth. You see, the Father is looking for such people to worship Him. God is a spirit, and those who worship Him must worship in spirit and in truth."

The woman said to Him, "I know that the promised Savior" (who is called Christ) "is coming. When He comes, He'll tell us everything."

"I am He — I who am talking to you," Jesus told her.

Just then His disciples came and were surprised to find

Him talking to a woman. But none of them asked, "What do You want?" or, "Why are You talking to her?"

Then the woman left her water jar and went back into the town. "Come," she told the people, "see a Man who told me everything I've done. Could He be the promised Savior?" They left the town and were coming to Him.

Meanwhile the disciples were urging Him, "Master, eat."

He told them, "I have food to eat which you don't know about."

"Could anyone have brought Him something to eat?" the disciples asked one another.

"My food is to do what He wants who sent Me," Jesus told them, "and to finish His work.

"Don't you say, 'Four more months and we'll cut the grain'? I tell you, look and see how the fields are white and ready to be cut. Already the reaper is getting paid and is gathering grain for everlasting life, so that the sower is happy with the reaper. Here the saying is true, 'One man sows, and another cuts the grain.' I sent you to cut grain where you had not worked before. Others have done the hard work, and you have succeeded them in their work."

Many Samaritans in that town believed in Him because the woman had declared, "He told me everything I've done." When the Samaritans came to Him, they asked Him to stay with them. And He stayed there two days. Then many more believed because of what He said. "We no longer believe on account of what you said," they told the woman. "Now we heard Him ourselves and know He certainly is the Savior of the world."

After two days He left.

Return to Galilee

With the power of the Spirit Jesus went back to Galilee. Now, when He came to Galilee, the people in Galilee welcomed Him. They had seen all He did at the festival in Jerusalem, since they too had gone to the festival. The news about Him spread all over the surrounding country.

He taught in their synagogs and began to preach God's good news: "The time has come, and God's kingdom is here. Repent, and believe the good news." And everybody praised Him.

An Officer's Son

Then Jesus went again to Cana in Galilee, where He had changed water to wine.

One of the king's officers lived at Capernaum. Now, his son was sick. When he heard Jesus had come from Judea to Galilee, he went to Him and asked Him to come down and heal his son, who was dying.

"If you don't see wonderful proofs and miracles," Jesus told him, "you won't believe."

"Lord, come down," the officer asked Him, "before my little boy dies."

"Go," Jesus told him, "your boy is well." The man believed what Jesus told him and left.

On his way back his slaves met him and told him his boy was well. So he asked them what time he got better. They told him, "Yesterday at seven in the evening the fever left him." Then the father knew it was the same hour when Jesus had told him, "Your boy is well." And he and everybody at his house believed.

This was the second miracle Jesus did after He had come from Judea to Galilee.

Nazareth Rejects Jesus

Then Jesus came to Nazareth, where He had been raised. On the Sabbath He went into the synagog as He used to do. He got up to read and was given the scroll of the prophet Isaiah. Unrolling the scroll, He found the place where it says:

The Spirit of the Lord is on Me because —
He anointed Me
   To tell the poor the good news.
He sent Me
   To announce to prisoners, "You are free,"
      to the blind, "You will see again,"
   To free those who are broken down,
   To announce a season when the Lord welcomes
      people.[49]

He rolled up the scroll, gave it back to the attendant, and sat down. Everybody in the synagog was watching Him closely as He said, "Today, while you're listening, what is written here has come true."

All spoke well of Him and were surprised to hear the beautiful words flowing from His lips. "Isn't this Joseph's son?" they were asking.

He answered them: "You will undoubtedly quote to Me the proverb 'Doctor, heal yourself!' and say, 'We've heard about everything You did in Capernaum. Do the same here in Your hometown.' I tell you," He added, "it is true no prophet is accepted in his hometown or honored in his own country.

"Let Me tell you this truth: There were many widows in Israel in the days of Elijah, when it didn't rain for three years and six months and there was a big famine all over the country. But Elijah wasn't sent to anyone except *a widow at Zarephath in the territory of Sidon.*[50] And there were lepers in Israel at the time of the prophet Elisha. But no one except *Naaman* from Syria *was made clean.*" [51]

As they were listening, all in the synagog became furious. They got up, pushed Him out of the town, and took Him to a brow of the hill on which their town was built, to hurl Him down the cliff. But He walked right through them and went away.

At Home in Capernaum

Leaving Nazareth, Jesus went down and made His home in Capernaum, a town by the lake in Galilee, in the area of Zebulun and Naphtali. And so what the prophet Isaiah said was to come true:

> Land of Zebulun and land of Naphtali,
> The way to the sea, across the Jordan,
> Galilee of the Gentiles!
> The people sitting in the dark will see a great light.
> For those sitting in the land of the shadow of death a light will rise.[52]

"Follow Me"

As He was walking along the shore of the Lake of Galilee, He saw two brothers, Simon, also called Peter, and his brother Andrew (who were fishermen), casting a net into the lake. "Come, follow Me," Jesus told them, "and I will make you fishers of men."

Immediately they left their nets and went with Him.

He went on a little farther and saw two other brothers, James, Zebedee's son, and his brother John. They were in their boat with their father Zebedee, mending their nets. Then He called them, and immediately they left the boat and their father Zebedee with the hired men in the boat and followed Him.

Jesus Drives Out a Devil

Then they went to Capernaum. The next Sabbath Jesus went into the synagog and began to teach. His teaching amazed the people because He taught them as one who had authority and not like the Bible scholars.

There was in their synagog just then a man with a spirit of an unclean devil. And he screamed out loud, "Oh, leave us alone, Jesus from Nazareth! You've come to destroy us! I know who You are — God's Holy One."

Jesus talked sharply to him: "Be quiet, and come out of him." The unclean spirit threw the man into convulsions, hurled him into the crowd, and with a loud shriek came out of him without doing him any harm.

They were all so amazed they argued with one another: "What kind of speaking is this? A new teaching! With authority and power He gives orders to the unclean spirits, and they obey Him and out they go."

So the news about Him quickly spread everywhere in all the surrounding country of Galilee.

Peter's Mother-in-Law

Right after leaving the synagog they went into the home of Simon Peter and Andrew. James and John went with them.

There Jesus saw Simon's mother-in-law down in bed with a high fever. And so the first thing they did was to ask Him to help her.

He went to her and, bending over her, ordered the fever to leave, took her hand, and helped her get up. The fever left her, and immediately she got up and waited on them.

In the evening, when the sun had gone down, the whole town had gathered at His door. All who had sick ones suffering from various diseases brought them to Him. He laid His hands on each of them and made them well. The people brought Him many who were plagued by devils. He drove out the spirits by talking to them. The devils went out of many, screaming, "You're God's Son." He talked sharply to them and wouldn't let the devils go on talking, because they knew He was the promised Savior. In this way what the prophet Isaiah said was to come true, *He took away our sicknesses and carried our diseases.*[53]

Preaching in Galilee

In the morning, long before daylight, Jesus got up and went out to a lonely place, and there He prayed. Simon and those who were with him searched for Jesus. When they found Him, they told Him, "Everybody's looking for You."

"Let us go somewhere else," He told them, "to the small towns that are near, so that I may preach there too. That's why I've come."

The crowds were looking for Him. When they came to Him, they tried to keep Him from leaving them. But He said to them, "I have to tell the good news of God's kingdom also in other towns. That's what I was sent to do."

Then He went around everywhere in Galilee, teaching in their synagogs, preaching the good news of the Kingdom, healing every kind of disease and sickness among the people, and driving out the devils.

The news about Him spread all over Syria. And the people brought to Him all who were suffering from various diseases and were in great pain, those who were plagued by devils, the epileptics, and the paralyzed, and He made them well.

Fishers of Men

One day Jesus was standing by the Lake of Galilee, and the people were crowding Him as they were listening to God's Word. He saw two boats on the shore of the lake. The fishermen had stepped out of them and were washing their nets. So Jesus got into one of the boats (it belonged to Simon) and asked him to go out a little way from the shore. Then He sat down and taught the people from the boat.

When He had stopped speaking, He told Simon, "Take the boat out where the water is deep, and let down your nets for a catch."

"Master," Simon answered, "we've worked hard all night and caught nothing. But if You say so, I'll let down the nets."

When the men had done this, they caught a very large number of fish, and their nets started to tear. So they waved to their partners in the other boat to come and help them. They came, and now they filled both boats so that they started to sink.

When Simon Peter saw this, he fell down at Jesus' knees. "Leave me, Lord," he said. "I'm a sinful man." He and all who were with him were amazed to see the fish they had caught, and so were James and John, Zebedee's sons, who were Simon's partners.

"Don't be afraid," Jesus told Simon. "From now on you're going to catch men."

So when they had brought the boats to the shore, they left everything and followed Him.

Jesus Heals a Leper

One day Jesus was in a town where there was a man who had leprosy all over his body. When he saw Jesus, the leper went to Him, bowed down to the ground before Him, and begged Him on his knees, "Lord, if You want to, You can make me clean."

Jesus felt sorry for him, stretched out His hand, and touched him. "I want to," He said. "Be clean!" Immediately the leprosy left him, and he was made clean.

Jesus sent him away with a stern warning: "Be careful not to say anything to anyone, but go, *let the priest examine* [54] you, and for your cleansing offer the sacrifices Moses ordered, to show them you're well."

But when he had left, he talked so much and spread the news about Jesus, that big crowds were gathering to hear Him and have their diseases healed. Jesus could no longer openly go into a town. He would go away to lonely places and pray. And still the people kept coming to Him from everywhere.

Jesus Forgives Sins

Some days later Jesus came again to His own town, to Capernaum, and people heard, "He's home."

One day, as He was teaching, so many gathered that there was no room even in front of the door. He was speaking the Word to them. Pharisees and Bible teachers were sitting there. They had come from every village in Galilee and Judea and from Jerusalem. And Jesus had the Lord's power to heal.

Then some people came and brought Him a paralyzed man lying on a bed, carried by four men. They tried to take him in and lay him in front of Jesus. But when they couldn't find a way to get him to Jesus on account of the crowd, they went up on the roof and opened up the roof over the place where Jesus was. Through the opening they had dug, through the tiles, they let down among the people, right in front of Jesus, the bed on which the paralytic was lying.

When Jesus saw their faith, He said to the paralytic, "Courage, son! Your sins are forgiven." Then the Bible scholars and the Pharisees began to question within themselves: "Why does He say this? Who is this fellow, talking such blasphemies? Who but God alone can forgive sins?"

Immediately Jesus knew in His spirit what they were thinking. "Why do you think evil in your hearts?" He asked them. "Is it easier to say to this paralyzed man, 'Your sins are forgiven,' or to say, 'Get up, take your bed, and walk'? I want you to know the Son of Man has power on earth to forgive sins." Then He said to the paralyzed man, "I tell you, get up, take your bed, and go home."

Immediately the man got up in front of them, took the bed he had been lying on, and went home, praising God.

When the crowd saw this, they were frightened. All were amazed and praised God for giving such power to men. Fearfully they declared, "You wouldn't believe what we've seen today! Never have we seen anything like this."

Matthew

Again Jesus went out along the lake. All the people were coming to Him, and He taught them.

As He passed by, He saw a tax collector by the name of Levi, also called Matthew, the son of Alphaeus, sitting in the tax office. "Come with Me," He told him. He got up, left everything, and went with Him.

Then Levi gave a big dinner for Him at his home. As Jesus was lying down to eat, a big crowd of tax collectors and sinners came and ate with Jesus and His disciples, because there were many who followed Him.

When the Pharisees and their Bible scholars saw Him eating with sinners and tax collectors, they complained to His disciples: "Why do you and your Teacher eat and drink with tax collectors and sinners?"

Jesus heard them and answered them: "Those who are healthy don't need a doctor, but the sick. Go and learn what this means: *I like mercy and not* mere *sacrifice.*[55] I didn't come to call righteous people but sinners to repent."

The Bridegroom

Then John's disciples and the Pharisees, who were fasting, came to Jesus. "John's disciples and the disciples of the Pharisees often fast and say prayers," they said to Him. "Why do Yours eat and drink?"

Jesus asked them, "Can you make the bridegroom's friends mourn and fast while the bridegroom is with them? As long as they have the bridegroom with them, they can't fast. The time will come when the bridegroom will be taken away from them, and in those days they will fast."

He pictured it to them in this way: "Nobody tears a piece of cloth from a new garment and sews it on an old garment. If you do, the new patch will tear away some of the old cloth, you'll tear the new cloth, and the hole will get worse; and the patch from the new won't match the old.

"Nobody pours new wine into old wineskins. If you do, the new wine will burst the skins and run out, and the wine and the skins will be lost. No, you pour new wine into fresh skins; then both are preserved.

"Nobody who has drunk old wine wants the new. 'The old tastes good,' he says."

Sick 38 Years

After this there was a Jewish festival, and Jesus went up to Jerusalem.

Near the Sheep Gate in Jerusalem there's a pool that the Jews call Bethesda. It has five porches. In them there used to lie a crowd of people who were sick, blind, lame, and paralyzed. * One man who was there had been sick thirty-eight years. Jesus saw him lying there and found out he had been sick a long time. "Would you like to get well?" He asked him.

"Lord," the sick man answered Him, "I don't have anybody to put me into the pool when the water is stirred. And while I'm trying to get there, somebody else steps in ahead of me."

"Get up," Jesus told him, "pick up your bed, and walk." Immediately the man got well, picked up his bed, and walked.

That day was a Sabbath. "Today is the day of rest," the Jews told the man who had been healed. "It's wrong for you to carry your bed."

He answered them, "The One who made me well told me, 'Pick up your bed and walk.'"

They asked him, "Who is the man that told you, 'Pick it up and walk'?" But the man who had been healed didn't know who He was, because Jesus had disappeared in the crowd that was there.

* Our oldest manuscripts, including Papyrus 75 and Papyrus 66, do not have John 5:3b-4: "waiting for the water to be stirred. At a certain time the Lord's angel would come down into the pool and stir the water. After the stirring of the water, the first to step in got well, whatever disease he was suffering from."

Later Jesus found him in the temple and said to him, "Look, you're well now. Don't sin anymore, or something worse may happen to you."

The man went back and told the Jews it was Jesus who made him well.

God's Son

Because Jesus was doing such things on a Sabbath, the Jews started to persecute Him. But Jesus answered them, "My Father has been working until now, and so I am working."

Then the Jews were all the more eager to kill Him, because He wasn't only abolishing the Sabbath but even calling God His own Father, making Himself equal to God.

"I tell you the truth," Jesus answered them, "the Son can do nothing by Himself but only what He sees the Father doing. You see, the Son does exactly what the Father does. The Father loves the Son and shows Him everything He is doing. And He will show Him even greater works than these so that you'll be surprised. As the Father wakes up the dead and makes them live, so the Son makes alive whom He wants to make alive.

"The Father doesn't judge anyone but has entrusted the judgment entirely to the Son so that all should honor the Son as they honor the Father. (Anyone who doesn't honor the Son doesn't honor the Father who sent Him. I tell you the truth: If you listen to what I say and believe Him who sent Me, you have everlasting life, and you will not be judged, but you have come from death to life.)

"Let me assure you, the hour is coming and is here now when the dead will hear God's Son calling them, and those who hear Him will live. As the Father has life in Himself, so He has given the Son the power of having life in Himself.

"He has also given Him power to judge because He is the Son of Man. This should not surprise you, because the hour is coming when all who are in their graves will hear Him calling and will come out. Those who have done good will rise to live; those who have done evil will rise to be condemned. I can do nothing by Myself. I judge only as I'm told to do, and so My judgment is just, because I'm not trying to do what I want but what He wants who sent Me.

"If I alone testify about Myself, My testimony isn't dependable. There's Someone else testifying about Me, and I know what He testifies about Me is true. You sent to John, and he testified to the Truth. Not that I get My testimony from a man, but I say this to save you. John was a lighted lamp that shone, and for a while you wanted to enjoy his light. But I have a greater testimony than John had. The works the Father gave Me to finish, these works that I do testify the Father sent Me. The Father who sent Me — He testified about Me. You never heard His voice or saw His form. You don't keep His Word within you, because you don't believe Him whom He sent. You search the Scriptures because you think you have everlasting life in them; and yet they testify about Me! But you don't want to come to Me to have life.

"I don't get glory from men. But I know in your hearts you don't love God. I have come in My Father's name, and you don't accept Me. If someone else comes in his own name, you'll accept him. How can you believe while you accept honor from one another but are not eager to have the honor that comes from the only God?

"Don't think that I will accuse you before the Father. There is already one who accuses you — Moses, whom you trust. If you really believe Moses, you would believe Me, because he wrote about Me. But if you don't believe what he wrote, how will you believe what I say?"

Lord of the Sabbath

At that time Jesus was going through the grainfields on a Sabbath. His disciples were hungry, and as they walked along, they were picking the heads of grain, rubbing them in their hands, and eating them.

When some of the Pharisees saw this, they asked Him, "Look, why are Your disciples doing something they shouldn't do on a day of rest?"

"Haven't you ever read what David did," Jesus asked them, "when he and his men were in need and got hungry — how he went into God's house when Abiathar was high priest and took the *loaves laid before God*,[56] which he and his men had no right to eat, but only the priests, and ate them and gave his men some too?

"Or haven't you read in the Law that the priests in the temple work on a Sabbath as on other days and yet do no wrong? I tell you, here is something greater than the temple. If you knew what this means, *I like mercy and not* mere *sacrifice*,[55] you would not have condemned the innocent."

Then He added, ("The Sabbath was made for man, not man for the Sabbath. The Son of Man is Lord also of the Sabbath.")

The Shriveled Hand

On another Sabbath Jesus again went into their synagog and taught. And there was a man whose right hand was shriveled. But the Bible scholars and the Pharisees were watching Jesus to see if He would heal him on a Sabbath.

"Is it right to heal on a Sabbath?" they asked Him. They wanted to find something to accuse Him of.

But He knew what they were thinking; so He said to the man with the shriveled hand, "Get up and come forward." The man got up and stood there.

"If anyone of you has only one sheep," Jesus asked them, "and it falls into a hole on a Sabbath, won't you take hold of it and lift it out? Now, isn't a man much more valuable than a sheep? I ask you, is it right on a Sabbath to do good or to do evil, to save a life or to kill? It is right, then, to do good on a day of rest!"

But they were silent. Looking around at all of them, He felt angry as well as sorry because their minds were closed. Then He told the man, "Stretch out your hand." He stretched it out, and his hand was made healthy again like the other hand.

But the Pharisees were furious and began to discuss with one another what they could do to Jesus. They left and immediately started plotting with Herod's men how to kill Him. Jesus knew about this, and so He left.

"My Servant"

Jesus went away with His disciples to the lake. Large crowds followed Him from Galilee and also from the whole country of Judea, Jerusalem, Idumea, the other side of the Jordan, the Ten-Towns, and the seacoast of Tyre and Sidon. They heard about everything He was doing and came to hear Him and have their diseases healed. He healed them all, also those who were plagued by unclean spirits. Whenever the unclean spirits saw Him, they would fall down before Him and yell, "You're God's Son!" But He strictly ordered them not to tell who He was.

All who had diseases rushed up to Him. All the people were trying to touch Him, because power came from Him and made them all well. To keep the crowd from crushing Him, He told His disciples to have a small boat ready for Him.

In this way what the prophet Isaiah said was to come true:

Here is My Servant whom I have chosen,
Whom I love and delight in.
I will put My Spirit on Him,
And He will announce justice to the nations.
He will not quarrel or shout.
Nor will anyone hear His voice in the streets.

He will not crush a bruised reed
Or put out a smoking wick
Till He has made justice victorious.
And His name will be the hope of the nations.[57]

Twelve Apostles

In those days, when Jesus saw the crowds, He went up the hill to pray, and He prayed to God all night.

When it was day, He sat down and called His disciples, those whom He wanted, and they came to Him. He chose twelve of them and called them apostles. He appointed them to be with Him and be sent out by Him to preach and have power to drive out devils. He appointed the twelve: first, Simon, whom He also gave the name Peter, and his brother Andrew; James, Zebedee's son, and John, the brother of James — He also gave these the name Boanerges, which means "thunderbolts"; Philip and Bartholomew; Matthew, the tax collector, and Thomas; James, the son of Alphaeus, and Thaddaeus (Judas, the son of James); Simon, called Zealot; and Judas, the man from Kerioth, who became a traitor.

He went down with them and stood on a level place with a big crowd of His disciples.

Sermon on the Mount

HAPPY PEOPLE

Jesus looked at His disciples and began to teach them:
"Happy are those who are *poor in spirit* [58] —
    they have the kingdom of heaven.
Happy are *those who mourn* —
    they will *be comforted.*[59]
Happy are you who are crying now —
    you will laugh.
Happy are *those who are gentle* —
    they *will own the land.*[60]

Happy are those who now hunger and thirst to be righteous —
they will be satisfied.

Happy are *those who are merciful —
they will find mercy.*[61]

Happy are *those whose hearts are pure* [62] —
they will see God.

Happy are those who make peace —
they will be called God's sons.

Happy are those who are persecuted for doing right —
they have the kingdom of heaven.

Happy are you when people hate you, exclude you from their company, insult you, persecute you, reject your name as evil, lie and tell only evil about you on account of Me. On that day be glad and dance with delight, because you have a great reward in heaven. You see, that's how their fathers treated the prophets who were before you. But —

Woe to you who are rich —
you've had your comfort.

Woe to you who are well fed now —
you will be hungry.

Woe to you who are laughing now —
you will mourn and cry aloud.

Woe to you when everybody speaks well of you —
that is how their fathers treated the false prophets."

SALT AND LIGHT

"You are the salt of the world. If salt loses its taste, how will it be made salty again? It's no longer good for anything but to be thrown out and trampled on by people.

"You are the light of the world. A town can't be hid when it's built on a hill. You don't light a lamp and put it in a cellar or under the peck measure but on the lampstand so that those who come in will see it shine. And it gives light to everybody in the house.(So let your light shine before people that they may see the good you do and praise your Father in heaven.")

JESUS KEEPS THE LAW

"Don't think that I came to set aside the Law or the prophets. I didn't come to set them aside but to fulfill them. I tell you the truth, till heaven and earth pass away, not an *i* or the dot of an *i* of the Law will pass away till everything is done. Anyone, then, who sets aside one of the least of these commandments and teaches others to do the same will be called the least in the kingdom of heaven. But anyone who does and teaches what they say will be called great in the kingdom of heaven. I tell you, unless your righteousness is much better than that of the Bible scholars and Pharisees, you will never get into the kingdom of heaven."

DON'T KILL

"You have heard that long ago the people were told: 'Don't kill.[63] Whoever kills must answer for it in court.'

"But I tell you, anyone who is angry with his brother must answer for it in court. Anyone who calls his brother an 'empty-head' must go before the highest court. Anyone who calls him a 'fool' must go into hellfire.

"So if you're bringing your gift to the altar and remember there that your brother has something against you, leave your gift there before the altar and go. First make up with your brother, and then come and offer your gift.

"If someone wants to sue you, be quick to make up with him while you are still on the way with him, or your accuser will hand you over to the judge, and the judge to the officer, and you will be put in prison. I tell you the truth, you will never get out until you pay the last cent."

DON'T LUST

"You have heard it was said: 'Don't commit adultery.' [64]
"But I tell you, anyone who looks at a woman to lust

after her has already committed adultery with her in his heart.

"If your right eye causes you to sin, tear it out and throw it away. It is better for you to lose a part of your body than to have all of it thrown into hell. And if your right hand causes you to sin, cut it off and throw it away. It is better for you to lose a part of your body than to have all of it go to hell.

"It was said: 'Anyone who divorces his wife *must give her a divorce paper.*' [65] But I tell you, anyone who divorces his wife, except for her being sexually unfaithful, makes her a partner in adultery. And also the man who marries the divorced woman is living in adultery."

DON'T SWEAR

"Again, you have heard that long ago the people were told: '*Don't swear to a lie,*' [66] and: '*Give the Lord what you swear to give Him.*' [67]

"But I tell you, don't swear at all, not by *heaven* — it *is God's throne;* or by *the earth* — it *is His footstool;* [68] or by Jerusalem — *it is the city of the great King.*[69] And don't swear by your head, because you can't make one hair white or black. Just say, 'Yes, yes; no, no.' Anything more comes from the evil one."

LOVE YOUR ENEMIES

"You have heard it was said, '*An eye for an eye, and a tooth for a tooth.*' [70]

"But I tell you, don't oppose an evil man. If anyone slaps you on your right cheek, turn and offer him the other cheek. If anyone wants to sue you for your shirt, let him have your coat too. If anyone takes your coat, don't stop him from taking your shirt. If anyone makes you go one mile, go two miles with him.

"If anyone asks you for anything, give it to him, and when anyone wants to borrow from you, don't turn away. And if anyone takes what is yours, don't insist on getting it back.

"You have heard it was said, '*Love your neighbor,*'[71] and hate your enemy.'

"But I tell you who are listening, love your enemies, be kind to those who hate you, bless those who curse you, and pray for those who insult you and persecute you. In this way you will show you are sons of your Father in heaven. He makes His sun rise on people whether they are bad or good and lets rain fall on them whether they do right or wrong.

"If you love those who love you, what's your reward? Don't tax collectors do that too? Even sinners love those who love them. If you treat only your brothers kindly, are you doing anything extraordinary? Don't the people of the world do that too? If you help those who help you, how should anyone be especially pleased with you? Sinners do that too. If you lend anything to those from whom you expect to get something, how should anyone be especially pleased with you? Sinners also lend to sinners to get back what they lend. No, love your enemies, help them, and lend to them without expecting to get anything back. Then you will have a great reward and will be the sons of the most high God, since He is kind to people who don't thank Him and are wicked. Be merciful as your Father is merciful. *Be perfect* [72] as your Father in heaven is perfect."

DON'T BLOW YOUR HORN

"Be careful not to do your good works before people to be seen by them. If you do, your Father in heaven will not reward you. So when you give to the poor, don't blow your horn, as hypocrites do in the synagogs and on the streets to be praised by people. I tell you, that's really all the reward they'll get. When you give to the poor, don't let your left hand know what your right hand is doing, that your giving may be secret. Then your Father, who sees what is secret, will reward you.

"When you fast, don't look sad like hypocrites. They disfigure their faces to show people they are fasting. I tell you, that's really all the reward they'll get. But when you fast, anoint your head, and wash your face so that nobody will see you fasting except your Father, who is with you when you're alone. And your Father, who sees what is secret, will reward you."

"When you pray, don't be like hypocrites, who like to stand praying in synagogs and on street corners in order to be seen by people. I tell you, that's really all the reward they'll get. But when you pray, *go into your own room, shut your door, and pray* [73] to your Father, who is with you when you're alone, and your Father, who sees what is secret, will reward you.

"When you pray, don't say meaningless words, like pagans, who think they'll be heard if they talk a lot. Don't be like them. Your Father knows what you need before you ask Him.

"This is how you should pray:

Our Father in heaven —
May Your name be kept holy,
Your kingdom come,
And Your will be done on earth as it is done in heaven.
Give us today our daily bread.
And forgive us our sins as we have forgiven those who
     sin against us.
And don't bring us into temptation,
But deliver us from evil.*

"If you forgive the sins of others, your Father in heaven will forgive you. But if you don't forgive the sins of others, your Father will not forgive your sins.

"Suppose one of you has a friend," Jesus said to His disciples, "and you go to him at midnight and ask him, 'Friend, lend me three loaves. A friend of mine on a trip has dropped in on me, and I have nothing to serve him.' Will he answer from within, 'Don't bother me. The door is already locked,

---

* The doxology is found in later manuscripts: "You are the King who rules with power and glory forever. Amen."

and my children are with me in bed. I can't get up and give you anything'? I tell you, although he won't get up and give you anything even though he's your friend, yet because you persist, he'll get up and give you anything you need.

"So I tell you: Ask and it will be given to you. Search and you will find. Knock and the door will be opened for you. Anyone who asks receives; anyone who searches finds; and anyone who knocks, the door will be opened for him.

"If your son asks you, his father, for bread, will any of you give him a stone? Or if he asks for a fish, will you give him a snake instead of a fish? Or if he asks for an egg, will you give him a scorpion? Now if you, bad as you are, know enough to give your children good gifts, how much more will your Father in heaven give the Holy Spirit and other good things to those who ask Him?"

TREASURES

"Don't store up for yourselves treasures on earth,
  Where moth and rust destroy them
  And thieves break in and steal.

"But store up for yourselves treasures in heaven,
  Where no moth or rust destroys them
  And no thieves break in and steal.

Where your treasure is, there your heart will be.

"Your eye is the lamp of your body. When your eye is healthy, you have light for your whole body. But when your eye is bad, your whole body will be dark. How dark it is when the light in you is dark! Then see to it that the light in you isn't dark. Now if you have light for your whole body and no part of it is dark, it will all have light just as when a lamp shines brightly on you.

"Nobody can serve two masters. Either he will hate the one and love the other or be loyal to the one and despise the other. You can't serve God and money."

DON'T WORRY

"So I tell you, don't worry about what you'll eat or drink to keep alive or what you'll wear on your bodies. Isn't life more than food, and the body more than clothes?

"Look at the birds in the air. They don't sow or cut grain or gather anything into barns; but your Father in heaven feeds them. Aren't you worth more than they?

"Can any of you by worrying add anything to your life?

"And why worry about clothes? See how the flowers grow in the field, and learn from them. They don't work and they don't spin. Yet, I tell you, even Solomon in all his glory didn't dress like one of these. If that's how God dresses the grass in the field, which lives today and tomorrow is thrown into a stove, how much more certainly will He put clothes on you — who trust Him so little?

"Don't worry, then, and say, 'What are we going to eat?' or, 'What are we going to drink?' or, 'What are we going to wear?' The people of the world run after all these things. Your Father in heaven knows you need them all. First be eager to have God as your King and His righteousness, and you'll get all these other things too.

"So, don't worry about tomorrow. Tomorrow will take care of itself. Each day has enough trouble of its own."

CRITICIZE YOURSELF

"Don't judge, and you will not be judged. The way you judge others, you'll be judged. Don't condemn, and you will not be condemned. Forgive, and you will be forgiven. Give, and it will be given you. A good measure, pressed together, shaken down, and running over, will be put into your lap. You see, the measure you use will be used for you."

He pictured it to them in this way: "Can a blind man lead another blind man? Won't they both fall into a ditch? A pupil is not above his teacher. But anyone who is well trained will be like his teacher.

"And why do you look at the speck in your brother's eye and don't notice the log in your own eye? How can you say to your brother, 'Brother, let me take the speck out of your eye,' as long as you don't see the log in your own eye? You hypocrite, first throw the log out of your own eye. Then you'll see clearly enough to take the speck out of your brother's eye."

PEARLS TO PIGS

"Don't give anything holy to the dogs or throw your pearls to the pigs, or they'll trample them under their feet and then turn and tear you to pieces."

THE GOLDEN RULE

"Do for others everything you want them to do for you. That is the Law and the prophets."

THE NARROW GATE

"Go through the narrow gate. The gate is wide, and the way is broad that leads to destruction, and many are going that way. But the gate is small, and the way is narrow that leads to life, and only a few are finding it."

FALSE PROPHETS

"Beware of false prophets. They come to you dressed like sheep, but in their hearts they're greedy wolves.

"You will know them by what they do. Every tree is known by its fruit. Can we pick grapes or figs from thornbushes and from thistles? No, every good tree bears good fruit, and a bad tree bad fruit. A good tree cannot bear bad fruit, or a bad tree good fruit. Any tree that doesn't bear good fruit is cut down and thrown into the fire. So you will know them by what they do.

"A good man produces good things from the good stored in his heart, and an evil man produces evil from his evil stored there. What you say flows from your heart.

"Why do you call Me Lord, Lord, but don't do what I tell you? Not everyone who calls Me Lord, Lord, will get into the kingdom of heaven, only he who does what My Father in heaven wants. Many will say to Me on that Day, 'Lord, Lord, didn't we *prophesy in Your name*,[74] drive out devils in Your name, and do many miracles in Your name?' Then I will tell them frankly, 'I never knew you. *Get away from Me, you who are so busy doing wrong.*'"[75]

BUILD ON A ROCK

"I will show you what kind of man anyone is who comes to Me and hears and does what I say. He's like a man who had the sense to build his house on a rock. He dug deep and laid the foundation on a rock. The rain poured down, and there was a flood. The torrents came, the winds blew, and they dashed against that house. But they couldn't move it, because it was built right. It didn't go down, because its foundation was on the rock.

"Everyone who hears what I say but doesn't do it is like a man who was so foolish he built his house, without a foundation, on sand. The rains poured down, the torrents came, the winds blew, and they dashed against that house. That house immediately collapsed and went down with a big crash."

HIS AUDIENCE

When Jesus finished all He had to say, the crowds who heard Him were amazed at His teaching. He taught them with authority and not like their Bible scholars.

He went down the hill, and large crowds followed Him.

· 4 ·

Second and Third Tour of Galilee

A Believing Captain

Then He went to Capernaum. There a certain captain's slave was sick. He was dear to him and now he was dying. The captain heard about Jesus and sent some Jewish elders to tell Him, "Lord, my slave is lying paralyzed at home. He's suffering terribly," and to ask Him to come and save his slave's life. They came to Jesus and earnestly pleaded with Him, "He deserves to have You do this for him, because he loves our people and built the synagog for us."

"I will go and make him well," Jesus said. So He went with them.

He wasn't far from the house when the captain sent friends to tell Him, "Lord, don't bother. I'm not good enough for You to come under my roof. And so I didn't think I was fit to come to You either. But just say a word, and my slave will be made well. I'm only a man who has to obey others, but I have soldiers under me. I tell one, Go, and he goes. And another, Come, and he comes. And my slave, Do this, and he does it."

Surprised to hear this, Jesus turned to the crowd following Him. "I tell you the truth," He said, "not even in Israel have I found such faith. I also tell you, many will come *from the east and the west* [76] and will eat with Abraham, Isaac, and Jacob in the kingdom of heaven, but those who were born to be the heirs of the kingdom will be thrown out into the dark. There they will cry and grind their teeth."

"Go," Jesus told the captain. "Let it be as you believed." And the slave was made well in that hour. When the men who had been sent went back to the house, they found the slave well again.

Jesus Raises a Widow's Son

Soon after this, Jesus went to a town called Nain, and His disciples and a large crowd went with Him. As He came near the gate of the town, a dead man was carried out. He was his mother's only son, and she was a widow. A big crowd from the town was with her.

When the Lord saw her, He felt sorry for her. "Don't cry," He told her.

He went up to the open coffin and touched it, and the men who were carrying it stood still. "Young man," He said, "I tell you, wake up." The dead man sat up and started to talk. And Jesus *gave him to his mother*. [77]

They were all overawed and praised God. "A great prophet has risen among us," they said, and, "God has come to help His people." This story about Jesus spread all over the country of the Jews and in all the surrounding territory.

John Sends Two Disciples

John's disciples told him in prison about all the works of Christ. Then John called two of his disciples and sent them to ask the Lord, "Are You the One who is coming, or should we look for someone else?"

The men came to Jesus and said, "John the Baptizer sent us to ask You, 'Are You the One who is coming, or should we look for someone else?' "

Just then He had healed many people of their diseases, ailments, and evil spirits and had given sight to many who were blind.

"Go," Jesus answered them, "tell John what you hear and see: *The blind see,* the lame walk, lepers are made clean, the *deaf hear,* the dead are raised, and *the poor hear the good news* [78] — and happy is anyone who doesn't turn against Me."

About John

When John's messengers had left, Jesus talked to the crowds about John:

"What did you go out into the wilderness to see — a reed shaken by the wind? What, then, did you go out to see — a man dressed in soft robes? Those who wear fine clothes and live in luxury you'll find in the palaces of kings.

"What, then, did you go out to see — a prophet? Let Me assure you, far more than a prophet. All the prophets and the Law prophesied up to the time of John, but he (are you willing to accept it?) is the Elijah who has to come. This is the one of whom it is written, '*I will send My messenger ahead of You to prepare* Your *way before* [79] You.' I tell you the truth, there never has appeared a woman's son greater than John the Baptizer. Yet the least in the kingdom of heaven is greater than John. If you can hear, listen!

"By letting John baptize them, all the people who heard him, even the tax collectors, admitted that God was right. But the Pharisees and the learned men of the Law, by not letting John baptize them, rejected what God had planned for them. From the time of John the Baptizer till now the kingdom of heaven has been suffering violence, and violent men are trying to take it by force.

"How should I picture the people of this age? What are they like? They're like little children sitting in the marketplace and calling to one another, 'We played a tune on the flute for you, but you didn't dance. We sang a funeral song, but you didn't beat your breasts and weep.' John the Baptizer has come; he doesn't eat bread or drink wine, and you say, 'There's a devil in him!' The Son of Man has come; He eats and drinks, and you say, 'Look at the glutton and drunkard, the friend of tax collectors and sinners!' And yet wisdom is shown to be right by all her children."

"She Loved Much"

One of the Pharisees invited Jesus to eat with him. He went into the Pharisee's home and lay down for the meal.

In the town there was a sinful woman. When she found out He was eating at the Pharisee's home, she brought a flask of perfume and stood behind Him at His feet. She was weeping and started to wet His feet with her tears. Then with the hair of her head she dried His feet, kissed them, and poured perfume on them.

The Pharisee who had invited Jesus saw this and said to himself, "If He were a prophet, He would know who is touching Him and what kind of woman she is. She's a sinner."

"Simon," Jesus answered him, "I have something to tell you."

"Say it, Teacher," he said.

"Two men owed a moneylender some money: One owed him five hundred denarii, and the other fifty. When they couldn't pay it back, he was kind enough to cancel the debt for both of them. Now, which of them will love him more?"

"I suppose," Simon answered, "the one who had the bigger debt canceled."

"You're right," Jesus told him. Then, turning to the woman, He said to Simon, "You see this woman? I came into your home, and you gave Me no water for My feet, but she wet My feet with her tears and dried them with her hair. You gave Me no kiss, but ever since I came in, she hasn't stopped kissing My feet. You poured no oil on My head, but she poured perfume on My feet. That's why I tell you her sins are forgiven, many as they are. You see, she has loved much. Of course, he to whom little is forgiven loves only a little."

Then He said to her, "Your sins are forgiven." His fellow guests began to ask among themselves, "Who is This that He should even forgive sins?"

Jesus said to the woman, "Your faith saved you. Go in peace!"

Through Galilee

After this Jesus traveled from one town and village to another, preaching and telling the good news of God's kingdom. The twelve were with Him. Also some women who had been healed of evil spirits and diseases: Mary, also called the woman from Magdala (seven devils had gone out of her); Johanna, the wife of Herod's manager Chusa; Susanna; and many other women. They supported Jesus and His disciples with their property.

Power over the Devil

Then Jesus came home. Again such a crowd gathered that Jesus and those with Him couldn't eat. When His family heard about it, they went to take charge of Him, because they were saying, "He's out of His mind!"

At that time some people brought to Jesus a man who had a devil and was blind and couldn't talk. He drove out the devil and healed the speechless man so that he could talk and see.

The people were all amazed. "Could this be the Son of David?" they asked. When the Pharisees (men trained in the Bible who had come down from Jerusalem) heard about it, they said, "Beelzebul is in Him," and, "He can drive out the devils only with the help of Beelzebul, who rules over the devils."

Knowing what they were thinking, Jesus called them to Him and pictured it to them in this way: "How can the devil drive out the devil? If one part of a kingdom fights another, that kingdom can't stand; it loses its people, and one house falls on another. And if one part of any town or home fights another, it can never stand. And so if the devil rebels against himself and drives himself out, he's fighting against himself. He and his kingdom can't stand, but his end has come. I say this because you say Beelzebul helps Me drive out the devils. Now if Beelzebul helps Me drive out the devils, who helps your sons drive them out? That's why they'll be your judges. But if God's finger, if God's Spirit helps Me drive out the devils, then God's kingdom has come to you.

"When a strong man, completely armed, guards his palace, his property is not disturbed. How can anyone go into a strong man's house and take away his goods without first tying the strong man up? But when someone stronger than he attacks him and defeats him, he'll take away his whole armor, in which he trusted. After that he'll rob his house and divide the plunder.

"Anyone who's not with Me is against Me, and anyone who doesn't help Me gather scatters. So I tell you the truth: Anything that people do will be forgiven, their sins and their slanders, though they slander ever so much. But anyone who slanders the Holy Spirit will never be forgiven. Anyone who talks against the Son of Man will be forgiven, but anyone who talks against the Holy Spirit will not be forgiven in this world or the next. Yes, he is guilty of an everlasting sin." He said this because they had said, "The Spirit in Him is unclean."

"Either the tree is good, and then its fruit is good. Or the tree is bad, and then its fruit is bad. You can tell a tree by its fruit. Brood of snakes, how can you who are so evil say anything good? What you say flows from your hearts. A good man produces good things from the good stored in him, but an evil man produces evil from the evil stored in him. But I tell you, on Judgment Day people will have to give an account of every useless word they say. By your words you'll be acquitted, and by your words you'll be condemned."

The Sign of Jonah

Then, meaning to test Him, some Bible scholars and Pharisees demanded that He show them some wonderful proof from heaven. "Teacher," they said, "we want You to show us some wonderful proof."

As the people were crowding around Him, He said, "These people of our time are wicked and unfaithful. They're looking for a proof, but the only proof they'll get is the prophet Jonah. As Jonah became a proof to the people of Nineveh, so the Son of Man will be a proof to these people. As *Jonah was in the belly of the big fish three days,*[80] so the Son of Man will be in the bosom of the earth three days. The men of Nineveh will rise up in the Judgment with these people and condemn them, because they repented when Jonah preached; and here you see more than Jonah. The queen from the south will rise up in the Judgment with these people and condemn them, because she came from the ends of the earth to hear Solomon's wisdom; and here you see more than Solomon.

"When an unclean spirit comes out of a man, he goes through dry places looking for a place to rest but doesn't find any. Then he says, 'I'll go back to the home I left.' He comes and finds it empty, swept, and decorated. Then he goes and takes home with him seven other spirits worse than himself, and they go in and live there. In the end that man is worse than he was before. That's what will happen to the wicked people of today."

Jesus' Mother and Brothers

When Jesus said this, a woman in the crowd called loud to Him, "Happy is the mother who bore You and nursed You."

"Yes," He said, "but happy are those who listen to God's Word and keep it."

He was still talking to the people when His mother and His brothers came. They were standing outside wanting to talk to Him but couldn't get near Him on account of the crowd. So they sent someone to Him to ask Him to come out. The crowd sitting around Jesus told Him, "Your mother and Your brothers are standing outside and want to see You and talk to You."

"Who is My mother," He asked the man that told Him, "and who are My brothers?" Then looking around at those who sat in a circle around Him and pointing with His hand to His disciples, He said, "These are My mother and My brothers. If you hear what God says and do what God, My Father in heaven, wants, you are My brother and sister and mother."

The Sower

That same day Jesus left the house and sat down by the lake and began to teach. A big crowd was gathering, and people were coming to Him from every town. So many people gathered around Him that He stepped into a boat and sat in it on the lake, while all the people stood on the shore, facing the lake. Then He used parables to teach them many things.

"Listen!" He said as He taught them. "A sower went out to sow his seed. As he was sowing, some seed fell along the road and was trampled on, and the birds in the air came and ate it. Some seed fell on rocky ground, where it didn't have much soil. Because the soil wasn't deep, the seed came up quickly. When the sun rose, it was scorched, and because it had no moisture and had not taken root, it withered. Some seed fell among thorns, and the thorns grew up with it and choked it, and it produced no grain. But some seed fell on good ground. It came up, grew, and produced grain, some a hundred, some sixty, and some thirty times as much as was sown."

When He had said this, He called out, "You have ears to hear. Then listen!"

His disciples asked Him what this parable meant. "You don't understand this parable," He said to them. "Then how will you understand any parables?

"Listen to what the parable of the sower means. The seed is God's Word. The sower sows the Word.

"And the ones along the road where the Word is sown are those who hear the message of the Kingdom but don't understand it. As soon as they hear it, the devil comes and takes away the Word out of their hearts to keep them from believing and being saved.

"It is the same with those in whom the seed falls on rocky ground. As soon as they hear the Word, they welcome it with joy, but it doesn't take root in them. They believe for a while, but when the Word brings them trouble or persecution and they're tempted, they immediately desert.

"In others the seed falls among thorns. They hear the Word, but the worries of the world, the deceitful pleasure of riches, the pleasures of life, and the desires for other things come in and choke the Word, and it can't produce anything.

"But in others the seed falls on good ground. They are the ones who continue to hear and welcome and understand the Word and keep it in a good and honest heart. They go on faithfully producing good things, one a hundred, another sixty, and another thirty times as much as was sown."

Why Jesus Spoke in Parables

Jesus used many parables like these to speak the Word to the crowds as they were able to hear it. He wouldn't tell them anything without a parable, so that what the prophet said would come true:

> *I will open My mouth to speak in parables,*
> *I will tell what has been hidden since the world was made.*[81]

But when He was alone with His disciples, He would explain everything to them.

Then the twelve and the others around Him asked Him, "Why are You talking to them in parables?"

"You are given the privilege to know the secrets of God's kingdom," He answered them, "but it isn't given to the others. To those on the outside I talk in parables because they see and yet don't see, and hear and yet don't hear or understand. In them more and more Isaiah's prophecy is coming true:

> *You will hear but never understand,*
> *You will look but never see.*
> *These people have become dull at heart and hard of hearing*
> *And have shut their eyes*
> *So that their eyes will never see, their ears never hear, or their hearts understand,*
> *And they will never turn to Me and let Me forgive and heal them.*[82]

"Happy are your eyes because they see and your ears because they hear. Let Me assure you, many prophets and righteous people longed to see what you see and didn't see it, to hear what you hear and didn't hear it.

"Nobody lights a lamp and hides it under a jar or puts it under a bed. No, you put it on a lampstand so that those who come in will see the light. Everything hidden will be uncovered, and every secret will be known and come to the light. If you have ears to hear, listen!

"Be careful, then, how you listen!" He told them. "The measure you measure with will be used for you. If you have something, you'll be given more, and so you'll get more and more. But if you don't have what you should have, even what you think you have will be taken away from you."

Growing by Itself

"God's kingdom," He said, "is like this: A man will sow seed on the ground. He will sleep through the night and get up for the day, and the seed will come up and grow, he doesn't know how. The ground by itself produces grain, first the green blade, then the head, then the full wheat in the head. When the grain is ready, he *swings the sickle, because it is time to cut the grain.*" [83]

Mustard Seed and Yeast

"What should we say God's kingdom is like," He asked, "or how should we picture it?" So He pictured it to them another way: "The kingdom of heaven is like a mustard seed a man took and planted in his garden. When sown on the ground, it's the smallest of all the seeds on earth. But when it's sown, it comes up and becomes the largest of all the garden plants. It becomes a tree and grows such large branches that *the birds in the air* can come and *nest in the shade of its branches.*" [84]

"With what should I compare God's kingdom?" He asked again. So He pictured it to them another way: "The kingdom of heaven is like yeast a woman took and mixed into a bushel of flour till it was all fermented."

Weeds in the Wheat

Jesus pictured it to them another way: "The kingdom of heaven is like a man who sowed good seed in his field. But while people were sleeping, his enemy came and sowed weeds among the wheat and went away. When the wheat came up and formed kernels, then the weeds showed up too.

"The owner's slaves came to him and asked him, 'Master, didn't you sow good seed in your field? Where did the weeds come from?'

" 'An enemy did that,' he told them.

" 'Do you want us to go and pull them out?' the slaves asked him.

" 'No,' he said, 'if you pull out the weeds, you may pull up the wheat with them. Let both grow together till the harvest. When the grain is cut, I will tell the reapers, "Gather the weeds first, and tie them in bundles to be burned, but bring the wheat into my barn." ' "

When Jesus had dismissed the people and gone into the house, His disciples came to Him and said, "Tell us what the parable of the weeds in the field means."

"The sower who sows the good seed," He answered, "is the Son of Man. The field is the world. The good seed are the sons of the kingdom. The weeds are the sons of the evil one. The enemy who sowed them is the devil. The harvest is the end of the world. The reapers are the angels. As the weeds are gathered and burned, so it will be at the end of the world. The Son of Man will send His angels, and they will take out of His kingdom *those who do wrong and all who lead others to do wrong* [85] and will throw them into the fiery furnace, where they will cry and grind their teeth. Then *the righteous will shine like* [86] the sun in their Father's kingdom. If you have ears, listen!"

Treasure, Pearl, and Fish

"The kingdom of heaven is like a treasure buried in a field. When a man found it, he buried it again and was so delighted with it he went and sold everything he had and bought that field.

"Here's another picture of the kingdom of heaven: A dealer was looking for fine pearls. When he found a very expensive pearl, he went and sold everything he had and bought it.

"Again, the kingdom of heaven is like a net that was let down into the lake, and it gathered all kinds of fish. When it was full they pulled it on the shore, sat down, and picked out the good fish and put them in containers but threw the bad ones away. So it will be at the end of the world. The angels will go out and separate the wicked from the righteous and throw them into the fiery furnace, where they will cry and grind their teeth.

"Did you understand all this?"

"Yes," they answered.

"And so every Bible student trained for the kingdom of heaven," He told them, "is like the owner of a house who brings out of his storeroom new things and old."

When Jesus had finished these parables, He left that place.

Wind and Water Obey

In the evening of that day, when Jesus saw a crowd around Him, He gave orders to cross to the other side. He and His disciples stepped into a boat. "Let us cross over to the other side of the lake," He said to them. Leaving the crowd behind, they took Jesus, just as He was, with them in the boat. There were other boats with Him. They started out. And as they were sailing along, He fell asleep.

Suddenly a violent storm hit the lake. It stirred the lake so that the waves dashed into the boat and were covering it; it was filling up fast, and they were in danger. Meanwhile, in the back of the boat, He was sleeping on the cushion.

So they went to Him and woke Him up. "Master, Master!" they called. "Save us! We're drowning! Don't You care?"

Then He got up and ordered the winds and the waves to stop. "Hush!" He said to the lake. "Be still!" And the wind quieted down, and it became very calm.

"Why are you such cowards?" He asked them. "Haven't you learned to trust yet?"

Frightened and amazed, the men asked one another, "What kind of man is He? He orders even the winds and the water, and they obey Him!"

The Gerasenes

They landed on the other side of the lake, in the country of the Gerasenes, which is opposite Galilee.

Just as He stepped out of the boat on the shore, two men with devils in them came out of the burial places and met Him. They were so savage nobody could go along that road.

One of the men was from the town. For a long time the unclean spirit had a firm hold on him. Nobody could bind him anymore, not even with a chain. He had often been bound with chains on hands and feet and had been kept under guard, but he had torn the handcuffs and ground to pieces the chains on his feet and was driven by the devil into lonely places. Nobody was strong enough to control him. He had worn no clothes for a long time. He wouldn't stay in a house but lived in these burial places. Always, day and night, he was shrieking in the burial places and in the hills and bruising himself with stones.

When he saw Jesus at a distance, he screamed, ran, bowed down before Him, and yelled at the top of his voice, "Let us alone, Jesus, Son of the most high God! Did You come here to torture us before it is time? I tell You by God, don't torture me." Jesus had been ordering the unclean spirit, "You unclean spirit, get out of the man."

"What is your name?" Jesus asked him.

"My name is Six Thousand," he told Him, "because we are many." Many devils had gone into him. They begged Him earnestly not to send them out of the country into the bottomless pit.

Far away a herd of many hogs was feeding on the hillside. "If You mean to drive us out," the devils were begging Jesus, "send us to the hogs; we want to go into them."

"Go," He told them.

The unclean spirits came out of the men and went into the hogs. Then the whole herd, about two thousand hogs, stampeded down the cliff into the lake and was drowned in the water.

But when those who had taken care of the hogs saw what had happened, they ran away and told everything in the town and in the country, especially about the men plagued by devils. Then the whole town came out to see what had happened. They came to Jesus and found the man from whom the legion of devils had gone out, now sitting dressed and in his right mind at Jesus' feet; and they were frightened. Those who had seen it told them how the man plagued by devils had been made well and about the hogs.

Then all the people of the surrounding country of the Gerasenes begged Jesus to leave them and their country, because terror had gripped them.

He got into a boat and started back. Now, the man from whom the devils had gone out begged Jesus to let him go with Him. But Jesus didn't let him. He sent him away and told him, "Go home to your people, and tell them how much the Lord God has done for you and how merciful He has been to you."

So the man left and began to tell publicly all over the town and in the Ten-Towns how much Jesus had done for him. And all were amazed.

Daughter of Jairus

When Jesus had again crossed over in the boat to the other side of the lake, a big crowd gathered around Him by the lake and welcomed Him, because they were all expecting Him. While He was talking to the people, a synagog leader by the name of Jairus came, and when he saw Jesus, he knelt at His feet and earnestly pleaded with Him to come to his home because his only daughter, about twelve years old, was dying. "My little daughter is dying," he said, "but come and lay Your hands on her so she will get well and live."

Jesus and His disciples got up and followed him. As He went, a big crowd followed Him and pressed Him on all sides and almost crushed Him.

Now there was a woman who had a flow of blood for twelve years. Nobody could cure her. She had suffered much under many doctors and had spent all she had. And she had not been helped at all but had actually gotten worse. Since she heard about Jesus, she came from behind in the crowd. "If I only touch His garment," she said to herself, "I'll get well," and she touched the tassel of His garment. Immediately her blood stopped flowing, and she felt in her body her trouble was gone and she was well.

At that moment Jesus felt power had gone from Him. Turning around in the crowd, He asked, "Who touched My clothes?"

When everybody denied having touched Him, Peter and His other disciples said to Him, "Master, You see how the people are crowding You and pressing against You, and You ask, 'Who touched Me?'"

But He was looking around to see her who had done this. "Somebody did touch Me," Jesus said. "I noticed that power went from Me."

When the woman saw she was discovered, she trembled with fear because she knew what had been done to her. She came, bowed down before Him, and in front of all the people told Him the whole truth, why she touched Him and how she was made well immediately.

"Cheer up, daughter," He told her, "your faith made you well. Go in peace, be healthy and rid of your trouble." After that the woman was well.

While He was still talking, some men came from the home of the synagog leader. "Your daughter died," they said. "Why trouble the Teacher anymore?"

Paying no attention to what they said, Jesus told the synagog leader, "Don't be afraid! Only believe, and she'll get well."

He let only Peter, James, and John, the brother of James, go with Him. So they came to the home of the synagog leader. There He saw the flute players and the noisy crowd, everyone crying, wailing aloud, and beating the breast, mourning her. "Why do you make a noise and cry?" He asked them when He came into the house. "Don't cry, but go away," He said. "The little girl isn't dead; she's sleeping."

They laughed at Him, because they knew she had died. But He put them all outside, took the child's father and mother and Peter, John, and James, and went in where the child was. He took the child's hand and called, "Talitha, * koom!" which means, "Little girl, I tell you, wake up!"

Her spirit returned, and immediately the girl got up and walked around. Then her parents were utterly amazed. Jesus ordered that she be given something to eat. He gave them strict orders not to tell anyone what had happened. But the news about this spread all over that part of the country.

Two Blind Men

When Jesus left that place, two blind men followed Him and called, "Have pity on us, Son of David."

* Talitha originally meant "lamb."

He went into a house, and there the blind men came to Him. "Do you believe I can do this?" Jesus asked them.

"Yes, Lord," they told Him.

Then He touched their eyes and said, "As you believed, so it must be done to you!" Then they could see again.

"See that nobody finds out about this!" He sternly ordered them. But they went out and spread the news about Him all over that part of the country.

A Dumb Man

As they were going out, a dumb man with a devil in him was brought to Him. But as soon as the devil was put out, the dumb man spoke.

The crowds were amazed and said, "We've never seen anything like this in Israel."

But the Pharisees declared, "The ruler of the devils helps Him drive out the devils."

Last Visit to Nazareth

Leaving that place, Jesus went to His hometown, and His disciples went with Him. When the Sabbath came, He taught the people in their synagog. Many who heard Him were amazed. "Where did He get this wisdom and the power to do these miracles?" they asked. "What is this wisdom given to Him? Such miracles His hands are doing! Isn't He the carpenter, the carpenter's and Mary's son, and a brother of James, Joseph, Judas, and Simon? And aren't all His sisters here with us? Where did He get all this?" So they turned against Him.

But Jesus told them, "A prophet is without honor only in his hometown, among his relatives, and in his family." Their unbelief amazed Him. It kept Him from doing many great works there. He couldn't do any miracle there except lay His hands on a few sick people and make them well.

Pray for Workers

Then Jesus traveled through all the towns and villages, teaching in their synagogs, preaching the good news of the Kingdom, and healing every disease and sickness.

As He saw the crowds, He felt sorry for them, because they were troubled and helpless *like sheep without a shepherd.*[87] Then He said to His disciples, "There's much grain to be harvested, but there are only a few workers. Ask the Owner of the crop to send out workers to bring in His grain."

Jesus Sends Out the Twelve

Jesus called His twelve disciples together and sent them out by twos, giving them power and authority to drive out all unclean spirits and heal every disease and sickness. He sent them to preach God's kingdom and heal the sick. Jesus sent the twelve out with the following instructions:

"Don't go among the Gentiles or into any town of the Samaritans. But go to the lost sheep of Israel. As you go, preach, 'The kingdom of heaven is here.' Heal the sick, raise the dead, cleanse lepers, drive out devils. Give these things as you received them — without pay.

"Don't take anything with you on the way except a stick — no gold, silver, or copper money in your pocket; no bread and no bag for the way. But have sandals strapped on your feet. And don't wear two tunics — a worker earns his keep.

"When you go into any town or village or home, look for a person there who is deserving, and stay with him till you leave. When you go into a home, greet it. If the home is deserving, let your peace come on it. But if it's unworthy, let your peace come back to you. If the people of any place don't welcome you or listen to what you say, leave that house or town, and shake the dust off the soles of your feet as a warning to them. I tell you the truth, on Judgment Day it will be easier for the land of Sodom and Gomorrah than for that town.

"You see, I'm sending you like sheep among wolves. So be shrewd as snakes and innocent as doves. Be on your guard against men, because they'll hand you over to their courts and whip you in their places of worship. On My account you'll be dragged before governors and kings to testify to them and to the nations. But when they hand you over to the authorities, don't worry how you'll speak or what you'll say. When the time comes, you'll be told what to say. It isn't you speaking but your Father's Spirit speaking through you.

"A brother will betray his brother to death, and a father his child. Children will *turn against*[88] their parents and kill them. Everybody will hate you because of My name. But be faithful to the end, and you will be saved. When they hunt you in one town, flee to another. Let Me assure you, before you have gone through all the towns of Israel, the Son of Man will come.

"A pupil isn't above his teacher, or a slave above his master. A pupil should be satisfied to share his teacher's lot and a slave to share his master's. If the master of the house was called Beelzebul, how much more certainly the members of his household! So, don't be afraid of them.

"All that's covered will be uncovered, and all that's hidden will be known. What I say to you in the dark, tell in the daylight; and what you hear whispered in your ear, preach from the housetops. Don't be afraid of those who kill the body and can't kill the soul, but fear Him who can destroy soul and body in hell. Aren't two sparrows sold for a cent? And not one of them will fall to the ground without your Father's permission. As for you, even the hairs on your head are all counted. So don't be afraid. You're worth more than many sparrows. Whoever will confess Me before other people, him will I confess before My Father in heaven. Whoever will deny Me before others, him will I deny before My Father in heaven.

"Don't think that I came to bring peace to the earth.

I didn't come to bring peace but a sword. I came to set *a man against his father, a daughter against her mother, a daughter-in-law against her mother-in-law. A man's enemies will be those in his own home.*[88] If you love father or mother more than Me, you're not worthy of Me; and if you love son or daughter more than Me, you're not worthy of Me. If you don't take your cross and follow Me, you're not worthy of Me. If you find your life, you'll lose it, but if you lose your life for Me, you'll find it.

"Anyone who welcomes you welcomes Me; and anyone who welcomes Me welcomes Him who sent Me. Anyone who welcomes a prophet because he is a prophet will get a prophet's reward. Anyone who welcomes a righteous man because he is righteous will get a righteous man's reward. Anyone who will give one of these little ones just a cup of cold water because he is My disciple, I tell you, will certainly not lose his reward."

After Jesus finished giving His twelve disciples these instructions, He went on from there to teach and preach in their towns. They left and went from village to village, and everywhere they preached that people should repent and told the good news. They also drove out many devils and poured oil on many who were sick and made them well.

Herod Kills John

Herodias had a grudge against John and wanted to kill him, but she couldn't do it. For although Herod also wanted to kill him, he was afraid of John because he knew John was a good and holy man, and he was afraid of the people because they considered John a prophet. So Herod protected him. When he listened to John, he was very much disturbed, and yet he liked to hear him.

An opportunity came on Herod's birthday, when he gave a dinner for his noblemen, the tribunes, and the leading men of Galilee. The daughter of Herodias came in and danced before them, and Herod and his guests were delighted with her. "Ask me for anything you want," the king told the girl, "and I'll give it to you." And he solemnly swore to her: *"I'll give you anything you ask, up to half of my kingdom."* [89]

She went out and asked her mother, "What should I ask for?"

"The head of John the Baptizer," her mother told her.

Urged on by her mother, she hurried right back to the king. "I want you to give me right now," she demanded, "here on a platter the head of John the Baptizer."

The king felt very sorry. But he had sworn to do it, and there were the guests — so he didn't want to refuse her. The king quickly sent a guard and ordered him to bring John's head and give it to her. He went and cut off John's head in prison. Then he brought the head on a platter and gave it to the girl. And the girl took it to her mother and gave it to her.

When John's disciples heard about it, they came and took his body and laid it in a grave. Then they went and told Jesus.

Has John Come Back?

At that time King Herod heard about everything Jesus was doing, because His name was now well known. Herod didn't know what to make of it and said, "I cut off John's head. Now who is this about whom I hear such things?"

Some people said, "John has risen from the dead." Others said, "He is Elijah." Still others, "He is a prophet like one of the other prophets." Still others, "One of the old prophets has risen."

But when Herod heard about it, he told his servants, "This is John the Baptizer! John, whose head I cut off, has risen from the dead, and that's why these powers are working in Him." And he wanted to see Jesus.

· 5 ·
Jesus Withdraws from Galilee

Looking for Rest

The apostles came back and gathered around Jesus. They reported to Him everything they had done and taught. "Now you come away to some deserted place," He told them, "where you can be alone, and rest a little." So many were coming and going there wasn't even time to eat.

When Jesus heard about John, He took the apostles away with Him in a boat, crossed over to the other side of the Lake of Galilee, which is the Lake of Tiberias, and came to a deserted place near a town called Bethsaida, in order to be alone. But many people heard of it or saw them leave and recognized them. And they ran there from all the towns and got there ahead of them. A large crowd was following Him because they saw the miracles He did on the sick.

When Jesus stepped out of the boat, He saw a big crowd and felt sorry for them because they were *like sheep without a shepherd.*[90] He welcomed them, began to teach them many things about God's kingdom, and healed those who needed healing.

Jesus Feeds Five Thousand

Jesus went up the hill and sat down there with His disciples. The Jewish festival of the Passover was near.

As Jesus looked up, He saw a large crowd coming to Him. When it was quite late in the evening, the twelve disciples came to Him. "This is a deserted place," they said, "and it's late. Send the crowd away to the villages and farms around us to get shelter and buy themselves something to eat."

"They don't need to go away," Jesus answered them. "You give them something to eat."

"Should we go and buy bread for two hundred denarii,"* they asked Him, "and give it to them to eat?"

He turned to Philip: "Where should we buy bread for these people to eat?" He asked this only to test him, since He knew what He was going to do.

"Two hundred denarii," Philip answered, "wouldn't buy enough bread for each of them to get just a little."

"How many loaves do you have?" He asked them. "Go and see."

They found out, and one of His disciples, Andrew, Simon Peter's brother, told Him, "There's a boy here who has five barley loaves and two fish. But what is that among so many? All we have is five loaves and two fish, unless perhaps we go and buy food for all these people."

"Let Me have them," He said.

Then He told His disciples, "Have the people all sit down on the green grass in groups of about fifty." There was much grass at the place. They did this and got them all seated in groups of hundreds and fifties.

* A denarius was a day's pay.

Then Jesus took the five loaves and the two fish and, looking up to heaven, gave thanks. Breaking the loaves, He gave them to the disciples to give to the people. The disciples gave them to the people. In the same way He also gave pieces of the two fish to everybody, as much as they wanted. All of them ate and had a hearty meal. When they had enough, He told His disciples, "Gather the pieces that are left so that nothing will be wasted." They gathered them and filled twelve baskets with the pieces that were left of the five barley loaves and of the fish.

Some five thousand men had eaten, not counting women and children. Seeing the miracle He did, the people said, "This certainly is the Prophet who is coming into the world."

Jesus Walks on Water

When Jesus learned that the people meant to come and take Him by force and make Him king, He quickly made His disciples get into the boat and cross over to Bethsaida ahead of Him; meanwhile He would send the people away. After saying good-by to them, He went up the hill to be alone and pray. When it got late, He was there alone.

His disciples went down to the lake, stepped into a boat, and were on their way across the lake to Capernaum. By this time it was dark, and Jesus hadn't come to them yet. A strong wind started to blow and stir up the lake. The boat was in the middle of the lake, many hundred yards from the shore. Jesus saw they were in great trouble from the waves as they rowed, because the wind was against them.

Toward morning, after they had rowed three or four miles, Jesus came to them, walking on the lake. He wanted to pass by them. When the disciples saw Him walking on the lake and coming near the boat, they were terrified. "It's a ghost," they said, and they cried out because they had all seen Him and were terrified.

Immediately He talked to them. "Have courage!" He said. "It is I. Don't be afraid."

They wanted to take Him into the boat. But Peter answered Him, "Lord, if it's You, order me to come to You on the water."

"Come," He said. So Peter got out of the boat, walked on the water, and went toward Jesus. But when he saw the wind, he was frightened and started to sink. "Lord, save me!" he cried.

Quickly Jesus stretched out His hand and caught him. "How little you trust Me!" He said to him. "Why did you doubt?"

When they stepped into the boat, the wind stopped. And the men in the boat bowed down before Him and said, "You certainly are God's Son." The disciples were completely dumfounded. They hadn't understood about the loaves. Their minds were dull.

And in a moment the boat came to the shore at Gennesaret, where they were going, and they anchored there.

Healings

As soon as they stepped out of the boat, the men of that place recognized Jesus and sent messengers all over that part of the country. People ran and started to carry all the sick on their beds to any place where they heard He was. And wherever He came — to villages, towns, or farms — they would lay down the sick in the public places and beg Him just to let them touch the tassel of His garment. And all who touched it were made well.

Bread from Heaven

The next day the people were still lingering on the other side of the lake. They had noticed only one boat was there and Jesus had not stepped into that boat with His disciples but they had gone away without Him. Other boats came from Tiberias near the place where they had eaten the bread after the Lord gave thanks. When the people saw that neither Jesus nor His disciples were there, they stepped into these boats and came to Capernaum, looking for Jesus. They found Him on the other side of the lake and asked Him, "Master, when did You get here?"

"Surely, I tell you," Jesus answered them, "you're not looking for Me because you've seen miracles but because you've eaten some of the bread and been well fed. Don't work for the food that spoils but for the food that keeps for everlasting life, which the Son of Man will give you because God the Father has sealed in Him the power to give it."

"What are the works God wants us to do?" they asked Him.

"What God wants you to do," Jesus answered them, "is to believe in Him whom He sent."

"What miracle can You do?" they asked Him. "Let us see it, and we'll believe You. What can You do? Our fathers ate the manna in the desert, as it is written: *He gave them bread from heaven to eat.*" [91]

"I tell you the truth," Jesus said to them, "Moses didn't give you the bread from heaven, but My Father gives you the real bread from heaven. God's bread is coming down from heaven and giving life to the world."

"Lord," they said to Him, "always give us this bread."

"I am the Bread of Life," Jesus told them. "Come to Me, and you will never be hungry. Believe in Me, and you will never be thirsty. But I have told you, 'You have seen Me, and you don't believe!' Everything the Father gives Me will come to Me, and anyone who comes to Me I will never turn away, because I came down from heaven, not to do what I want but what He wants who sent Me; and He who sent Me doesn't want Me to lose any of those He gave Me but to raise them on the last day. Yes, My Father wants everyone who sees the

Son and believes in Him to have everlasting life, and He wants Me to raise him on the last day."

Then the Jews grumbled because He said, "I am the Bread that came down from heaven." "Isn't this Jesus, Joseph's son," they asked, "whose father and mother we know? Then how can He say, 'I came down from heaven'?"

"Don't grumble among yourselves," Jesus answered them. "A person can come to Me only if the Father who sent Me draws him. Then I will raise him on the last day. The prophets wrote, *God will teach everyone*.[92] Everyone who listens to the Father and learns from Him comes to Me. Not that anyone has seen the Father; only He who comes from God has seen the Father. I tell you the truth, if you believe, you have everlasting life.

"I am the Bread of Life. Your fathers ate the manna in the desert, and they died. But this is the Bread coming down from heaven so that anyone may eat it and not die. I am the living Bread that came down from heaven. If anyone eats this Bread, he will live forever. The bread I'll give to bring life to the world is My flesh."

Then the Jews argued with one another: "How can He give us His flesh to eat?"

"I tell you the truth," Jesus answered them, "unless you eat the flesh of the Son of Man and drink His blood, you don't have any life in you. If you eat My flesh and drink My blood, you have everlasting life, and I will raise you on the last day. My flesh is a real food, and My blood is a real drink. If you eat My flesh and drink My blood, you stay in Me and I in you. As the living Father sent Me and I live because of the Father, so if you eat Me, you will live because of Me. This is the Bread that came down from heaven. It isn't like the bread the fathers ate. They died. Eat this Bread, and you will live forever."

He said this while He was teaching in a synagog in Capernaum. When they heard it, many of His disciples said, "This is hard to take. Who can listen to Him?"

Inwardly aware that His disciples were complaining about this, Jesus asked them, "Does this upset you? What if you see the Son of Man go up where He was before? The Spirit makes alive; the flesh doesn't help. The words I spoke to you are Spirit, and they are life. But some of you don't believe." Jesus knew from the beginning who wouldn't believe and who would betray Him. So He added, "That is why I told you a person can come to Me only if the Father gives him the power."

As a result many of His disciples went back to their old life and wouldn't go with Him anymore. Then Jesus asked the twelve, "Do you want to leave Me too?"

"Lord, to whom should we go?" Simon Peter answered Him. "You have words of everlasting life. And we have come to believe and know You are God's Holy One."

"Didn't I choose the twelve of you," Jesus asked, "and one of you is a devil?" He meant Judas, the son of Simon, the man from Kerioth. He was going to betray Him — one of the twelve.

Later Jesus went around in Galilee. He didn't want to travel in Judea because the Jews were trying to kill Him.

Unclean Hands

Then the Pharisees and some Bible scholars who had come from Jerusalem gathered around Jesus. They saw some of His disciples eat with unclean hands, that is, without washing them. (Now the Pharisees, like all other Jews, don't eat without washing their hands up to the wrist — to keep the rules handed down by their fathers. Coming from the marketplace, they don't eat without first washing; and there are many other rules they've learned to keep — baptizing cups, pitchers, copper pans, and couches.)

"Why do Your disciples sin against the rules handed down by our fathers?" the Pharisees and the Bible scholars asked Him. "They don't wash their hands when they eat."

"Why do you sin against God's commandment for the sake of your rules?" He asked them. "Hypocrites, Isaiah was right when he prophesied about you as it is written: *These people honor Me with their lips, but their hearts are far away from Me. They worship Me in vain because they teach men's rules.*[93] You give up God's commandment and keep men's rules."

He added: "You have a fine way of setting aside God's commandment in order to keep your rules! For example, God has said, *Honor your father and your mother,*[94] and, *Anyone who curses father or mother must die.*[95] But you say, 'If anyone says to his father or mother, "I'm giving God anything by which I might help you," he doesn't have to honor his father.' Then you don't let him do anything for his father or his mother anymore. In this way, by the rules you have taught you set aside what God has said. And you're doing many things like that."

Then He called the people again and told them, "Listen to Me, all of you, and understand this: Nothing that comes from the outside into a person's mouth can make him unclean, but what goes out of his mouth makes him unclean."

When He had left the people and gone home, the disciples came to Him. "Do you know the Pharisees were offended when they heard You say that?" they asked Him.

"Any plant My Father in heaven didn't plant," He answered, "will be torn out by the roots. Let them go; they are blind leaders. When one blind man leads another, both will fall into a ditch."

His disciples asked Him about the illustration. "Tell us what You mean by this illustration," Peter said to Him.

"Are you still as dull as the others?" He asked. "Don't you know that nothing coming from the outside into a person can make him unclean, because it doesn't go into his heart but into his stomach and so passes away?" (Here Jesus made all foods clean.) "But what goes out of the mouth comes from the heart, and that makes a person unclean. Yes, from within, out of men's hearts, come evil thoughts, sexual sins, stealing, murders, adulteries, greed, wickedness, cheating, lust, a jealous eye, lies, slanders, pride, foolishness. All these evils come from within and make a person unclean. But eating without washing your hands doesn't make you unclean."

A Non-Jewish Woman

Leaving that place, Jesus went away to the neighborhood of Tyre and Sidon. He went into a house and didn't want anyone to know it but couldn't keep it secret.

There was a Canaanite woman of that territory in whose little daughter there was an unclean spirit. The woman wasn't Jewish but was born a Phoenician in Syria. As soon as she heard about Him, she came out and was asking Him to drive the devil out of her daughter. "Have pity on me, Lord, Son of David!" she called. "A devil is making my daughter miserable."

But He didn't answer her a word. Then His disciples came to Him and urged Him, "Send her away. She's yelling after us."

"I was sent only to the lost sheep of Israel," He answered.

She came and bowed down at His feet. "Lord, help me!" she said.

"First let the children eat all they want," He answered her. "It isn't good to take the children's bread and throw it to the puppies."

"You're right, Lord," she answered Him, "but even the puppies under the table eat some of the children's crumbs that drop from their masters' table."

Then Jesus answered her, "O woman, you have a great faith! Because you said this, go! Let it be done for you as you wish. The devil has gone out of your daughter." At that moment her daughter was made well. The woman went home and found the little child lying on the bed and the devil gone.

A Deaf and Dumb Man

Jesus again left the country of Tyre and went through Sidon and the country of the Ten-Towns to the Lake of Galilee. Then He went up a hill and sat there.

Many people came to Him, bringing the lame, blind, crippled, deaf, and many others and laid them at His feet. He made them well, so that the people were surprised to find that the dumb talked, the cripple had sound limbs, the lame walked around, and the blind could see. And they praised the God of Israel.

Some people brought Him a man who was deaf and tongue-tied, and they urged Jesus to lay His hand on him. Taking him away from the crowd to be alone with him, He put His fingers into the man's ears. He spit and touched his tongue and looked up to heaven and sighed. Then He said to him, "Ephphatha!" which means, "Open!" His ears were opened, his tongue was set free to speak, and he talked naturally.

Jesus ordered the people not to tell anyone. But the more He forbade them, the more widely they spread the news. They were dumfounded. "He has done everything well," they said. "He even makes the deaf hear and the dumb speak."

Jesus Feeds Four Thousand

At that time there were again many people who had nothing to eat. So Jesus called His disciples. "I feel sorry for the people," He said. "They've been with Me three days now and have nothing to eat. I don't want to let them go home without eating; they may get exhausted on the way. Some of them have come a long way."

"Where could we get enough bread here in the wilderness to feed such a crowd?" His disciples asked Him.

"How many loaves do you have?" Jesus asked them.

"Seven," they said, "and a few small fish."

He ordered the people to sit down on the ground. Then He took the seven loaves, gave thanks, broke them, and gave them to His disciples to hand out, and they handed them to the people. They also had a few small fish. He blessed them and asked that these too be handed out. All of them ate and had enough. They picked up the pieces that were left — seven baskets full. Four thousand men had eaten, not counting women and children.

Then He dismissed the people.

A Proof from Heaven

Then Jesus and His disciples got into the boat and came into the neighborhood of Dalmanutha (or Magadan).

The Pharisees and Sadducees came and started to argue with Him. To test Him, they asked Him to show them some wonderful proof from heaven.

He answered them, "In the evening you say, 'The weather will be fine, because the sky is red.' And in the morning: 'There will be a storm today, because the sky is red and gloomy.' You know how to judge the appearance of the sky correctly but can't judge the signs of the times." *

With a deep sigh from His spirit He asked, "Why do the wicked and unfaithful people of today demand a proof? Surely, I tell you, the only proof they'll get is that of Jonah."

Then He left them and went away.

Yeast of the Pharisees

He got into the boat again and started to cross to the other side. When the disciples started out, they forgot to take bread and had only one loaf with them in the boat.

Then Jesus definitely warned them: "Beware of the yeast of the Pharisees and Sadducees and the yeast of Herod!"

* Jesus' words in this paragraph are omitted in some of our oldest manuscripts.

As they were arguing about this with one another, they mentioned, "We didn't take any bread."

Aware of what was going on, Jesus asked, "Why are you arguing about not having any bread? You have so little faith! Don't you know or understand yet? Are your minds closed? *You have eyes — don't you see? You have ears — don't you hear?* [96] And don't you remember? When I broke the five loaves for the five thousand, how many baskets full of pieces did you pick up?"

"Twelve," they told Him.

"And the seven loaves for the four thousand — how many baskets full of pieces did you pick up?"

"Seven," they answered Him.

"Don't you understand yet?" He asked them. "Why don't you see I wasn't talking to you about bread? But beware of the yeast of the Pharisees and Sadducees!"

Then they understood He didn't warn them against the yeast in bread but against the teaching of the Pharisees and Sadducees.

A Blind Man

So they came to Bethsaida. There people brought a blind man to Jesus and begged Him to touch him. He took the blind man's hand and led him out of the village. Then He spit on his eyes and laid His hands on him. "Can you see anything?" He asked him.

He looked up. "I see the people," he said. "They look to me like trees walking around."

When Jesus again laid His hands on his eyes, he saw distinctly; sight came back, and he saw everything clearly. Jesus sent him home, saying, "But don't go into the village."

"You Are the Son of God"

Then Jesus and His disciples went to the villages around Philip's Caesarea. On the way, once when He was praying and only His disciples were with Him, He asked them, "Who do people say I, the Son of Man, am?"

"Some say John the Baptizer," they answered Him. "Others say Elijah, still others Jeremiah, and still others that one of the old prophets has come back to life."

"But who do you say I am?" He asked them.

"You are the Savior whom God has sent," Simon Peter answered Him, "the Son of the living God!"

"Happy are you, Simon, son of John," Jesus answered him, "because no flesh and blood, but My Father in heaven has revealed this to you. I tell you, you are Peter, and on this rock I will build My church, and the forces of hell will not overpower it. I will give you the keys of the kingdom of heaven. Anything you bind on earth will be bound in heaven, and anything you free on earth will be freed in heaven."

Then He gave the disciples strict orders not to tell anyone that He was the promised Savior.

"I Will Die and Rise Again"

After this, Jesus Christ kept teaching His disciples: "The Son of Man has to go to Jerusalem, suffer much, be rejected by the elders, the ruling priests, and the Bible scholars, be killed, and then rise on the third day." He was speaking quite frankly.

But Peter took Him aside and started to correct Him, "God be merciful to You, Lord! This must never happen to You!"

Turning, He looked at His disciples and corrected Peter. "Get behind Me, devil!" He said. "You're tempting Me to sin, because you're not thinking what God thinks but what men think."

Take the Cross

Then Jesus called the people as well as His disciples and told all of them, "If you want to follow Me, deny yourself, take up your cross every day, and come with Me. If you want to save your life, you will lose it. But if you will lose your life for Me and for the good news, you will save it. What good does it do you to win the whole world and lose your life? Or what would you give to buy back your life? If among the unfaithful and sinful people of today you're ashamed of Me and what I say, then the Son of Man will be ashamed of you when He comes with His angels in His glory and the glory of the Father and the holy angels. Then *He will give each one according to what he has done.*[97]

"Let Me assure you," He told them, "there are some standing here who will never taste death till they see the Son of Man coming to rule as King, when God has come to rule with power."

Jesus Shows His Glory

About a week after He said this, Jesus took with Him Peter, James, and John, the brother of James, and led them up a high mountain to be alone with them and to pray. While He was praying, He was changed before them, His face shone like the sun, and His clothes became dazzling white — nobody on earth could bleach them so white. And there were two men talking with Him; they were Moses and Elijah. They appeared in glory and were talking about His leaving this world, which was to happen at Jerusalem.

But Peter and the men with him had been overcome by sleep. Waking up, they saw His glory and the two men standing with Him. When these were leaving Him, Peter said to Jesus, "Master, it's good for us to be here. If You wish, let's put up three shelters here, one for You, one for Moses, and one for Elijah." He didn't know what he was saying; they were so terrified.

He was still speaking when a bright cloud suddenly came and overshadowed them. They were frightened as they went into the cloud. Then a voice came out of the cloud: "This is

My Son whom I love and *delight in, whom I have chosen. Listen to Him."* [98]

When the disciples heard this, they fell down with their faces on the ground; they were terrified. But Jesus came and touched them. "Get up," He said, "and don't be afraid." Suddenly, as they looked around, they no longer saw anyone but Jesus with them.

On their way down the mountain Jesus ordered them, "Don't tell anyone what you have seen till the Son of Man has risen from the dead."

They kept silent and in those days told nobody anything of what they had seen. They kept in mind what He said and argued with one another, asking, "What is this rising from the dead?"

So the disciples asked Him, "Why, then, do those who know the Bible say, 'First Elijah has to come'?"

"First *Elijah* does come," He answered, "and *puts* everything *in order again.*[4] But I tell you Elijah has already come, and people didn't know him but treated him as they pleased, as it is written about him. And what is written about the Son of Man? That He must suffer much and be treated shamefully."

Then the disciples understood He was talking about John the Baptizer.

The Epileptic Boy

The next day, when they had come down from the mountain and got back to the other disciples, they saw a big crowd around them and some Bible scholars arguing with them. Then the whole crowd was amazed to see Jesus, and they ran and welcomed Him.

"What is this argument about?" He asked them.

Then a man in the crowd came to Jesus and knelt before Him. "Teacher," he said, "I brought You my son. I beg You, look at my son and have pity on him. He is my only child.

He's epileptic and very sick. There's a speechless spirit in him. Wherever the spirit takes hold of him, he suddenly shrieks. It throws him into convulsions, it throws him down; he foams at the mouth and grinds his teeth and gets rigid. It will hardly stop mistreating him. I brought him to Your disciples and asked them to drive out the spirit, but they couldn't make him well."

"O you unbelieving and perverted people!" Jesus answered. "How long must I be with you? How long must I put up with you? Bring him here to Me."

They brought the boy to Him. As soon as the spirit saw Jesus, it dashed the boy on the ground and threw him into convulsions. He fell on the ground and rolled around and foamed at the mouth.

Jesus asked his father, "How long has he been like this?"

"Since he was a child," he said. "It often threw him into fire or into water to kill him. Oh, if You can do anything, have pity on us and help us."

"You say, 'If You can'!" Jesus answered him. "Anything can be done if you believe."

Immediately the child's father cried out, "I do believe; help me with my unbelief."

When Jesus saw a crowd quickly gather around Him, He talked sharply to the unclean spirit: "You deaf and dumb spirit, I order you, 'Come out of him, and don't go into him again.'"

The devil screamed and wrenched him violently and came out of him. The boy became like a corpse, so that everybody said, "He's dead."

Jesus took his hand, helped him get up, and he stood up. After that the boy was well, and Jesus gave him back to his father. All were amazed to see God's wonderful power.

Afterwards, when Jesus went into a house and His disciples were alone with Him, they asked Him, "Why couldn't we drive out the spirit?"

"You have so little faith," He told them. "This kind can be

driven out only by prayer. I tell you the truth, if you have faith no bigger than a mustard seed, you will say to this mountain, 'Move from here to there,' and it will move. Then you can do anything."

"I Will Die and Rise Again"

Leaving that place, they started to go on byways through Galilee. Jesus didn't want anybody to know about it, because He was teaching His disciples.

While everybody thought how wonderful everything was that Jesus was doing and His disciples were getting together as a group, Jesus told them, "Listen carefully to what I say. The Son of Man is going to be betrayed into the hands of men, and they will kill Him, but on the third day after He's killed He will rise."

Then they felt very sad. But they didn't know what He meant. It was hidden from them so that they didn't understand it. And they were afraid to ask Him about it.

Coin in a Fish's Mouth

When they came to Capernaum, the collectors of the temple tax came to Peter. "Doesn't your Teacher pay the temple tax?" they asked.

"Certainly," he answered.

Peter went into the house, but before he could speak, Jesus asked him, "What do you think, Simon? From whom do the kings of the world collect toll or tax — from their children or from other people?"

"From other people," he answered.

"Then the children are free," Jesus told him. "But we don't want to give them a reason to think wrong of us. So go to the lake and throw in a hook. Take the first fish that comes up, open its mouth, and you will find a coin. Take that and give it to them for Me and you."

Who Is Greatest?

When He came home, He asked the disciples, "What were you discussing on the way?" They were silent because they had on the way discussed who was the greatest. But Jesus knew what they were thinking.

He sat down and called the twelve. They came to Him and asked, "Who is really the greatest in the kingdom of heaven?"

"If anyone wants to be first," He told them, "he will have to be last of all and serve everybody."

He called a little child, had him stand in front of them, put His arms around him, and said to them, "I tell you the truth, if you don't change and become like little children, you will never get into the kingdom of heaven. If you become humble like this little child, you are the greatest in the kingdom of heaven. And if you welcome a child like this in My name, you welcome Me. And if you welcome Me, you welcome not only Me but Him who sent Me. You see, if anyone is the least of all of you, he is great."

"He Is for Us"

"Teacher," John said to Jesus, "we saw a man driving out devils in Your name, and we tried to stop him because he hasn't been with us."

"Don't try to stop him," Jesus said. "Anyone who does a miracle in My name cannot turn around and speak evil of Me. Anyone who isn't against us is for us. I tell you, anyone who gives you a cup of water to drink because you belong to Christ will certainly not lose his reward."

Do I Lead Others to Sin?

Jesus told His disciples, "If anyone leads into sin one of these little ones who believe in Me, it would be better for him to have a big millstone hung around his neck and be drowned in the lake where it's deep. Woe to the world because it tempts people to sin! Temptations to sin must come, but woe to that man who tempts others to sin! Watch yourselves.

"If your hand makes you sin, cut it off and throw it away. It is better for you to go into life crippled than to have two hands and go to hell, where the fire can't be put out. If your foot makes you sin, cut it off and throw it away. It is better for you to go into life with only one foot than to have two feet and be thrown into the everlasting fire. If your eye makes you sin, tear it out and throw it away. It is better for you to go into life in God's kingdom with one eye than to have two eyes and be thrown into hellfire, where *the worm that consumes them doesn't die and the fire isn't put out.*[99]

"Everyone has to be salted with fire. Salt is good. But if salt loses its taste, how will you make it taste salty again? Keep salt within you, and so live in peace with one another.

"Be careful not to despise one of these little ones. I tell you their angels in heaven always see the face of My Father in heaven.

"What do you think? If a man has a hundred sheep and one of them gets lost, will he not leave the ninety-nine in the hills and go and look for the sheep that's wandering away? And if he finds it, I tell you he's certainly more delighted with it than with the ninety-nine that didn't get lost. So your Father in heaven doesn't want one of these little ones to be lost."

Tell Him His Fault

"If your brother sins against you, go, and when you're alone with him, show him how he is wrong. If he listens to you, you have won your brother. But if he won't listen, take one or two with you so that *you have two or three witnesses for everything.*[100] If he won't listen to them, tell it to the church. But if he won't even listen to the church, treat him like a pagan and a tax collector. I tell you the truth: Whatever you don't forgive on earth will not be forgiven in heaven, and whatever you forgive on earth will be forgiven in heaven.

"Again I tell you: If two of you here on earth agree to ask for anything, My Father in heaven will certainly do it for you. Where two or three have come together to be with Me, there I am among them."

Forgive!

Then Peter came to Jesus and asked Him, "Lord, how often do I have to forgive my brother who sins against me? Seven times?"

"I tell you," Jesus answered him, "not seven times but seventy times seven times. If your brother sins, correct him; and if he's sorry, forgive him. Even if he sins against you seven times in one day and seven times comes back to you and says, 'I'm sorry,' forgive him.

"That is why the kingdom of heaven is like a king who wanted to settle accounts with his slaves. When he began to do so, there was brought to him one who owed him ten thousand talents.* But he couldn't pay it, and so the master ordered him, his wife, his children, and all he had to be sold to pay the debt. Then the slave got down on his knees and, bowing low before him, begged: 'Be patient with me, and I'll pay you everything.'

"The master felt sorry for his slave, freed him, and canceled his debt. But when that slave went away, he found one of his fellow slaves who owed him a hundred denarii.† He grabbed him and started to choke him. 'Pay what you owe,' he said.

"Then his fellow slave got down on his knees and begged him, 'Be patient with me, and I'll pay you.' But he refused and went and put him in prison till he would pay what he owed.

* One "talent" of silver weighed about as much as 1,500 silver dollars.

† One denarius was a day's pay.

"When his fellow slaves saw what had happened, they felt very sad and went and told their master the whole story.

"Then his master sent for him. 'You wicked slave!' he said to him. 'I canceled all you owed me, because you begged me. Shouldn't you also have treated your fellow slave as mercifully as I treated you?' His master was so angry he handed him over to the torturers till he would pay all he owed him.

"That is what My Father in heaven will do to you if each of you will not heartily forgive his brother."

·6·
In Judea

To Jerusalem!

The Jewish festival of Booths was near. So His brothers told Jesus, "Leave this place, go to Judea, and there let Your disciples see the works You're doing. Nobody goes on doing things secretly when he wants to be known publicly. If You do these things, let the world see You." Not even His brothers believed in Him.

"It isn't the right time for Me yet," Jesus told them, "but any time is right for you. The world can't hate you, but it hates Me because I tell the truth about it that it is doing wrong. You go up to the festival. I'm not going up to this festival right now, because it isn't the right time for Me yet."

After telling them this, He did stay in Galilee. But as the time was coming nearer for Him to be taken up to heaven, He showed He was determined to go to Jerusalem. After His brothers had gone up to the festival, He left Galilee and went up too, not publicly but without being seen.

He sent messengers ahead of Him. They went and stopped in a village of the Samaritans to arrange a place for Him to stay. But the people didn't welcome Him, because He was going to Jerusalem. When His disciples James and John saw this, they asked, "Lord, do You want us to order *fire to come down from heaven and burn* [101] them up?"

But He turned and sternly corrected them. So they went on to another village.

"I Will Follow, but—"

As they were walking along the road, a man trained in the Bible came to Him and said, "Teacher, I will follow You anywhere You go."

"Foxes have holes," Jesus told him, "and birds in the air have nests, but the Son of Man doesn't have a place to lay His head."

He told another disciple, "Follow Me."

"Lord," that disciple said to Him, "first let me go and bury my father."

But Jesus told him, "Follow Me and let the dead bury their dead. But you go and tell about God's kingdom."

"I will follow You, Lord," said another, "but first let me say good-by to my people at home."

"Anyone who lays his hand on a plow," Jesus answered him, "and keeps looking back isn't fit for God's kingdom."

At the Festival of Booths

Then they went into the country of Judea on the other side of the Jordan.

So the Jews were looking for Jesus in the crowd at the festival. "Where is He?" they kept asking. And there was much whispering about Him in the crowds. "He's a good man," some said; but others, "No, He deceives the people." Yet nobody would talk about Him in public because everybody was afraid of the Jews.

But when the festival was already half over, Jesus went up to the temple and started to teach. The Jews were surprised. "How can He know so much," they asked, "when He hasn't been in the schools?"

"What I teach doesn't come from Me," Jesus answered them, "but from Him who sent Me. If anyone wants to do His will, he'll know whether My teaching is from God or I speak My own thoughts. Anyone who speaks his own thoughts tries to glorify himself. But He who wants to glorify the One who sent Him tells the truth, and there's nothing wrong in Him. Didn't Moses give you the Law? Yet none of you does what the Law tells you. Why do you want to kill Me?"

"There's a devil in You," the crowd answered. "Who wants to kill You?"

"I did one thing," Jesus answered them, "and you're all surprised about it. Moses gave you circumcision (not that it came from Moses but from our ancestors), and you circumcise a person on a Sabbath. If a child is circumcised on a day of rest to keep the Law of Moses, do you feel bitter toward Me because I made all of a man well on a Sabbath? Don't judge by what you see, but be fair when you judge."

Then some of the men from Jerusalem said, "Isn't He the man they want to kill? But here He speaks in public, and they don't say a thing to Him! Surely the rulers haven't found out He's the promised Savior, have they? Now, we know where this One comes from. But when the promised Savior comes, nobody knows where He's from."

"You know Me," Jesus called aloud as He was teaching in the temple, "and you know where I come from. I didn't by Myself decide to come, but there's One who is real who sent Me. You don't know Him, but I know Him because I come from Him and He sent Me."

Then they tried to arrest Him, but nobody laid a hand on Him, because the right time hadn't come yet for Him.

But many in the crowd believed in Him. "When the

promised Savior comes," they asked, "will He do more miracles than this One has done?"

The Pharisees heard the people muttering such things about Him. So the ruling priests as well as the Pharisees sent their men to arrest Him.

"I'll be with you just a little longer," said Jesus; "then I go to Him who sent Me. You'll be looking for Me and won't find Me; and where I am, you can't come."

The Jews asked one another, "Where's He intending to go, saying we won't find Him? He doesn't intend to go to our people scattered among the non-Jews and teach the non-Jews, does He? What does He mean by saying, 'You'll be looking for Me and won't find Me,' and, 'Where I am, you can't come'?"

On the last day, the great day of the festival, as Jesus was standing there, He called out loud, "If you're thirsty, come to Me and drink. If you believe in Me, streams of living water will flow from you, as the Bible has said." By this He meant the Spirit, whom those who believed in Him were to receive. The Spirit hadn't come yet, because Jesus hadn't been glorified yet.

After they heard Him say this, some of the people said, "This is certainly the Prophet." Others said, "This is the promised Savior." Still others asked, "What! Does the promised Savior come from Galilee? Doesn't the Bible say, 'The promised Savior *will come from the descendants of David* and *from* the little town of *Bethlehem*,[102] where David lived'?" So the people were divided over Him. Some of them wanted to arrest Him, but nobody laid hands on Him.

When the men who had been sent went back to the ruling priests and Pharisees, these asked them, "Why didn't you bring Him?"

"Nobody ever spoke like this Man," the men answered.

"You haven't been deceived too, have you?" the Pharisees asked them. "No ruler or Pharisee has believed in Him, has he? But this crowd, which doesn't know the Bible, is cursed."

One of them, Nicodemus, who had once come to Jesus, asked them, "Does our Law condemn anyone without first hearing what he has to say and finding out what he's doing?"

"Are you from Galilee too?" they asked him. "Search and see; the Prophet doesn't come from Galilee."

Then everyone went home. But Jesus went to the Mount of Olives.

The Adulteress*

Early in the morning He came back into the temple. All the people came to Him, and He sat down and taught them.

The Bible scholars and the Pharisees brought to Him a woman who had been caught in adultery and had her stand in the middle. "Teacher," they told Him, "this woman was caught in the act of adultery. In the Law, Moses ordered us to stone such women. Now, what do You say?" They asked this to test Him. They wanted to find something to accuse Him of.

Jesus bent down and with His finger wrote on the ground. But when they kept on asking Him, He got up. "Anyone that's without sin among you," He said, "should be the first to throw a stone at her." Then He bent down again and wrote on the ground.

Convicted by their conscience as they heard Him, they went out one by one, beginning with the older men, till all had gone and Jesus was left alone with the woman in the middle of the place. Jesus got up. "Woman, where are they?" He asked her. "Didn't anyone condemn you?"

"No one, Lord," she said.

"I don't condemn you either," Jesus said. "Go; from now on don't sin anymore."

* Our best manuscripts, including the two oldest papyri (P66 and P75, dated about A. D. 200), omit this story and the two sentences just before it. It is most likely a true story in the life of Jesus but not a part of the Gospel that John wrote.

Jesus Argues with the Jews

Jesus spoke to them again, "I am the Light of the world. Follow Me, and you will never wander in the dark but will have the Light of Life."

"You testify about Yourself," the Pharisees said to Him. "We can't depend on Your testimony."

"Even if I testify about Myself," Jesus answered them, "you can depend on My testimony, because I know where I came from and where I'm going; but you don't know where I came from or where I'm going. You judge in a human way, a way in which I don't judge anybody. But whenever I judge, you can depend on My judgment because I am not alone, but I'm with the Father who sent Me. In your own Law it is written the testimony of two men is valid. I testify about Myself, and the Father who sent Me testifies about Me."

"Where is Your Father?" they asked Him.

"You don't know Me or My Father," Jesus answered. "If you knew Me, you would know My Father."

He said this in the room of the treasury while He was teaching in the temple; nobody arrested Him, because the right time hadn't come yet for Him.

"I'm going away," He said to them again, "and you'll be looking for Me, but you will die in your sin. Where I'm going, you can't come."

"Is He going to kill Himself?" the Jews asked. "Is that what He means when He says, 'Where I'm going, you can't come'?"

"You're from below," He told them. "I'm from above. Your home is in this world. My home is not in this world. That's why I told you, 'You will die in your sins'; if you don't believe I'm the One, you will die in your sins."

"Who are You?" they asked Him.

"What should I tell you first?" Jesus asked them. "I have much to say about you and to condemn. But I tell the world only what I heard from Him who sent Me, and He tells the truth." They didn't understand He was talking to them about the Father.

So Jesus told them, "When you have lifted up the Son of Man, you will know I am the One and I do nothing by Myself, but I speak as My Father taught Me. And He who sent Me is with Me and has not left Me alone, because I always do what pleases Him."

As He was saying this, many believed in Him. Then Jesus said to those Jews who believed in Him, "If you live in My Word, you are really My disciples, and you will know the truth, and the truth will free you."

"We are Abraham's descendants," they answered Him, "and have never been anybody's slaves. How can You say, 'You'll be freed'?"

"I tell you the truth," Jesus answered them, "everyone who lives in sin is a slave to sin. A slave doesn't stay in the home forever. A son stays forever. If, then, the Son frees you, you will really be free. I know you're Abraham's descendants. But you want to kill Me because My Word is not working in you. I'm telling what I've seen, being with My Father, and you do what you've heard from your father."

"Abraham is our father," they answered Him.

"If you were Abraham's children," Jesus told them, "you would do what Abraham did. But now you want to kill Me, a Man who told you the truth, which I heard from God. Abraham didn't do that. You're doing what your father does."

"We weren't born outside of marriage," they said. "God alone is our Father."

"If God were your Father," Jesus told them, "you would love Me because I came from God, and as such I am here. I did not by Myself decide to come, but He sent Me. Why don't you understand what I say? Because you can't listen to what I tell you. Your father is the devil, and you want to do what your father wants. From the beginning he has been murdering people and hasn't stood in the truth, because there's no truth in him. When he tells a lie, he's telling it from his heart, because he's a liar and the father of lies. Now, because I tell the truth, you don't believe Me. Which of you can prove Me guilty of a sin? If I tell the truth, why don't you believe Me? A child of God listens to what God says. You don't listen to Him because you're not God's children."

"Aren't we right," the Jews answered Him, "when we say You're a Samaritan and there's a devil in You?"

"There's no devil in Me," Jesus answered, "No, I honor My Father, but you dishonor Me. I'm not trying to get glory for Myself. There's One who wants Me to have it, and He's the Judge. Let me assure you: If you keep My Word, you will never see death."

"Now we know there's a devil in You," the Jews told Him. "Abraham died, and so did the prophets, but You say, 'If you keep My Word, you will never taste death.' Are You greater than our father Abraham? He died, and the prophets died. Who do You think You are?"

"If I glorify Myself," Jesus said, "My glory is nothing. It is My Father who glorifies Me, He of whom you say, 'He's our God.' You don't know Him, but I know Him. And if I would say I don't know Him, I'd be a liar like you. But I do know Him, and I obey His Word. Your father Abraham was delighted to know of My day; he saw it and was glad."

"You're not fifty years old yet," the Jews said to Him, "and Abraham has seen You?"

"I tell you the truth," Jesus told them, "I was before Abraham."

Then they picked up stones to throw at Him. But Jesus hid Himself and left the temple.

A Blind Man Sees

As Jesus was passing by, He saw a man who had been blind from his birth. "Master," His disciples asked Him, "why was he born blind? Did he sin or his parents?"

"Neither he nor his parents," Jesus answered. "He is blind

to show what God can do with him. We must do the works of Him who sent Me while it is day. The night is coming when nobody can work. As long as I'm in the world, I'm the Light of the world."

After He said this, He spit on the ground and with the spit made some mud and put the mud on the man's eyes. "Go," He told him, "wash in the pool of Siloam" (the name means "sent"). He went and washed. And as he walked away, he could see.

Now, his neighbors and others who used to see him as a beggar asked, "Isn't this the man who used to sit and beg?"

"It is he," some said. Others said, "No, but he looks like him." But he himself said, "I'm the one."

Then they asked him, "How did you get your sight?"

"The man they call Jesus made some mud," he answered, "and put it on my eyes and told me, 'Go to Siloam and wash.' So I went and washed, and then I could see."

"Where is He?" they asked him.

"I don't know," he answered.

They brought him who had been blind to the Pharisees. Now, it was a Sabbath when Jesus made the mud and gave him his sight. So the Pharisees also asked him how he got his sight.

"He put mud on my eyes," the man told them, "and I washed them, and now I can see."

"This Man is not from God," said some of the Pharisees, "because He doesn't rest on a Sabbath." Others asked, "How can a sinful man do such miracles?" So they disagreed.

Then they asked the blind man again, "What do you say about Him, since He gave you your sight?"

"He's a prophet," he answered.

The Jews didn't believe the man had been blind and got his sight till they called the parents of the man who could see now. "Is this your son who you say was born blind?" they asked them. "How does it happen he can see now?"

"We know he's our son," his parents answered, "and was

born blind. But we don't know how it is he can see now or who gave him his sight. Ask him; he's of age. He'll tell you about himself." His parents said this because they were afraid of the Jews. The Jews had already agreed to put out of the synagog anyone who confessed Jesus was the promised Savior. That is why his parents said, "He's of age; ask him."

So once again they called the man who had been blind. "Give glory to God," they told him. "We know this Man is a sinner."

"I don't know if He's a sinner," he answered. "I know only one thing — I used to be blind, and now I can see."

"What did He do to you?" they asked him. "How did He give you your sight?"

"I've already told you," he answered them, "and you heard it. Why do you want to hear it again? You don't want to be His disciples too, do you?"

"You're His disciple," they answered him scornfully, "but we're Moses' disciples. We know God spoke to Moses, but this Fellow — we don't know where He's from."

"Well, that's strange!" the man answered them. "You don't know where He's from, and yet He gave me my sight. We know that God doesn't hear sinners but hears anyone who worships God and does what He wants. Nobody has ever heard of anyone giving sight to a man born blind. If this One were not from God, He couldn't do anything."

"You were altogether born in sins," they answered him, "and are you trying to teach us?" Then they put him out of the synagog.

Jesus heard they had put him out. Finding him, He asked him, "Do you believe in the Son of Man?"

"Who is He, sir?" he asked. "I want to believe in Him."

"You've seen Him," Jesus told him. "It is He who is now talking to you."

"I do believe, Lord," he said and bowed down to worship Him.

Then Jesus said, "I've come into this world to judge men,

so that those who don't see may see and those who see may turn blind."

Some Pharisees who were near Him heard this. "We aren't blind, are we?" they asked Him.

"If you were blind," Jesus told them, "you wouldn't be sinning. But now you say, 'We see,' and you go on sinning."

The Good Shepherd

"I tell you the truth: The man who doesn't come into the sheepfold through the door but climbs over somewhere else is a thief and a robber. But the one who comes in through the door is the shepherd of the sheep. The doorkeeper opens the door for him, and the sheep listen to his voice. He calls his own sheep by their names and leads them out. When he has brought out all his own sheep, he walks ahead of them, and the sheep follow him because they know his voice. They will not follow a stranger but will run away from him because they don't know the voice of strangers."

This was the illustration Jesus used in talking to them, but they didn't know what He meant. So Jesus spoke again: "I tell you the truth: I am the Door for the sheep. All who came before Me were thieves and robbers, but the sheep didn't listen to them. I am the Door. If anyone comes in through Me, he will be saved and will go in and out and find pasture.

"A thief comes only to steal and kill and destroy. I came so that they will have life and have it overflowing in them. I am the Good Shepherd. The Good Shepherd gives His life for the sheep. When a hired man, who isn't a shepherd and doesn't own the sheep, sees a wolf coming, he leaves the sheep and runs away — and the wolf carries them off and scatters them — because he works for money and doesn't care about the sheep. I am the Good Shepherd, and I know My own and My own know Me, as the Father knows Me and I know the Father. And I give My life for the sheep. I have other sheep too, that are not in this fold. I must lead those too, and they will listen to My voice, and so they will become one flock with *One Shepherd*.[103] The Father loves Me because I give My life in order to take it back again. Nobody takes it from Me. No, of My own free will I am giving it. I have the power to give it, and I have the power to take it back again. This is what My Father ordered Me to do."

These words again caused a split among the Jews. Many of them said, "There's a devil in Him and He's crazy. Why do you listen to Him?" Others said, "Nobody talks like this when there's a devil in him. Can a devil give sight to the blind?"

Seventy-two Missionaries

After this the Lord appointed seventy-two others and sent them out by twos to go ahead of Him to every town and place where He intended to go.

"There's much grain to be cut, but there are only a few workers," He told them. "Ask the Owner of the crop to send out workers to bring in His grain. Go! I'm sending you like lambs among wolves. Don't carry a purse, a bag, or shoes, and don't stop to greet anyone on the way. When you go into a house, say first, 'May there be peace in this house.' If a man of peace lives there, your peace will rest on him; but if not, it will come back to you. Stay in that house and eat and drink whatever they have, since a worker earns his pay. Don't move from one house to another. When you go into any town and the people welcome you, eat what they serve you. Heal the sick that are there, and tell the people, 'God's kingdom has come close to you!'

"But if you go into a town and they don't welcome you, go out on its streets and say, 'The dust of your town has clung to our feet — we're wiping it off in protest against you! But realize this: God's kingdom has come near you!' I tell you, on that Day it will be easier for Sodom than for that town."

Then He began to denounce the cities where He had

done most of His miracles, because they had not repented: "Woe to you, Chorazin! Woe to you, Bethsaida! If the miracles done in you had been done in Tyre and Sidon, they would long ago have repented, sitting in sackcloth and ashes. I tell you, on Judgment Day it will be easier for Tyre and Sidon than for you. And you, Capernaum, will you be *lifted up to heaven? You will go down to hell!* [104] If the miracles that have been done in you had been done in Sodom, it would still be there today. I tell you, on Judgment Day it will be easier for the country of Sodom than for you.

"Anyone who hears you hears Me, and anyone who rejects you rejects Me. But anyone who rejects Me rejects Him who sent Me."

The seventy-two came back delighted. "Lord," they said, "even the devils do what we tell them in Your name."

"I watched the devil fall from heaven like lightning," He told them. "You know, I've given you the power to *step on snakes* [105] and scorpions and to trample on all the enemy's power, and nothing will hurt you. Only don't be glad that the spirits obey you but that your names are written in heaven."

In that hour the Holy Spirit filled Jesus with joy. "I praise You, Father, Lord of heaven and earth," He said, "for hiding these things from wise and intelligent people and uncovering them for little children. Yes, Father, I praise You for wanting it to be that way.

"My Father put everything in My hands. Only the Father knows the Son. And only the Son — and anyone to whom the Son wants to reveal Him — knows the Father."

Turning to His disciples, He said to them alone, "Happy are the eyes that see what you see. I tell you, many prophets and kings longed to see what you see but didn't see it, and hear what you hear but didn't hear it.

"Come to Me, all you who are working hard
    and carrying a heavy load,
And I will give you rest.

Take My yoke on you and learn from Me —
I am gentle and humble-minded —
Then *you will find your rest.*[106]
My yoke is easy,
And My load is light."

The Good Samaritan

Then an expert in the Law came forward to test Jesus. "Teacher," he asked, "what do I do to get everlasting life?"

"What is written in the Law?" Jesus asked him. "What do you read there?"

"*Love the Lord your God with all your heart,*" he answered, "*and with all your life and with all your strength* [107] and with all your mind, and *your neighbor like yourself.*" [108]

"You're right," Jesus told him. "*Do that and you will live.*" [109]

But he wanted to justify himself. So he asked Jesus, "And who is my neighbor?"

Jesus went into the matter and said:

"A man going from Jerusalem down to Jericho fell into the hands of robbers. They stripped him, struck him blow after blow, and went away leaving him half dead.

"Just at that time a priest happened to go along that road, but when he saw him, he passed by on the other side. So did also a Levite who came to the place: he looked at him and passed by on the other side.

"Then a Samaritan, as he was traveling, came near him, and when he saw him, he felt sorry for him. He went to him and bandaged his wounds, pouring on oil and wine. Then he put him on his own animal, brought him to an inn, and took care of him. The next day he took out two denarii and gave them to the innkeeper. 'Take care of him,' he said, 'and anything else you spend on him I'll repay you when I come back.'

"Which of those three, do you think, was a neighbor to the man who had fallen into the hands of the robbers?"

"The one who was kind enough to help him," he said.
"Go and do as he did," Jesus told him.

Mary Listens to Jesus

As they were walking along, Jesus came to a village where a woman by the name of Martha welcomed Him to her home. She had a sister by the name of Mary. She sat down at Jesus' feet and listened to what He said.

But Martha was worried about all she had to do for them. So she came and asked, "Lord, don't You care that my sister has left me and I have to do the work alone? Now tell her to help me."

"Martha, Martha," the Lord answered her, "you worry and fuss about a lot of things. But there's only one thing you need. Mary has made the right choice, and it must not be taken away from her."

The Lord's Prayer

Once Jesus was praying in a certain place. When He stopped, one of His disciples asked Him, "Lord, teach us to pray as John taught his disciples."

He told them, "When you pray, say:

'Father, may Your name be kept holy,
Your kingdom come,
Your will be done on earth as it is in heaven.
Give us every day our daily bread.
Forgive us our sins, as we too forgive everyone who sins
    against us.
And don't bring us into temptation.' "

Warnings

Jesus had been speaking, when a Pharisee invited Him to eat at his home. So He went in and lay down to eat. But the Pharisee was surprised to see He didn't wash before the meal.

The Lord said to him, "You Pharisees keep cleaning the outside of the cup and of the dish, but inside you're full of greed and wickedness. You fools, didn't He who made the outside make the inside too? Just give your heart in helping the poor, and you'll find everything clean.

"But woe to you Pharisees! You give a tenth of mint, rue, and every vegetable, and you fail to be just and to love God. You should have done these without neglecting the others.

"And woe to you Pharisees! You like to have the seats of honor in the synagogs and to be greeted in the marketplaces. Woe to you! You're like the unmarked graves people walk over without knowing what they are."

"Teacher," one of the men of the Law said to Him, "when You say that, You insult us too."

"Woe also to you experts in the Law!" He said. "You load people with burdens they can hardly carry, but not with one finger will you touch these burdens yourselves. Woe to you! You build monuments for the prophets your fathers murdered. So you are witnesses and approve of what your fathers did. They murdered them, and you just build something. That's why God's wisdom has said: I will send them prophets and apostles, and they will murder or persecute some of them so that the people of today may be punished for the blood of all the prophets poured out since the world was made, from the blood of Abel to the blood of Zachariah, who was killed between the altar and the temple. Yes, I tell you, the people of today will be punished for it.

"Woe to you experts in the Law! You've taken away the key to knowledge. You didn't go in yourselves and kept out those who tried to go in."

When Jesus went outside, the Bible scholars and the Pharisees fiercely opposed Him and cross-examined Him about many things, watching Him closely to trap Him in something He might say.

Don't Be Afraid of Men

When so many thousands of people came together that they trampled on one another, Jesus began to speak first to His disciples: "Beware of the yeast of the Pharisees — I mean, their hypocrisy. Everything that's covered will be uncovered, and every secret will be known. Everything you said in the dark will be heard in the light, and what you whispered in the ear in the inner rooms will be announced from the roofs. But I tell you, My friends, don't be afraid of those who kill the body and then can't do any more. I will point out the One you must fear. Fear Him who after killing you has the power to throw you into hell. Yes, I tell you, fear Him!

"Aren't five sparrows sold for two cents? And God doesn't forget any one of them. Why, even the hairs on your heads are all counted! Don't be afraid — you're worth more than many sparrows! I tell you, whoever will confess Me before other people, him the Son of Man will confess before God's angels. Anyone who denies Me before other people will be denied before God's angels. Anyone who will speak against the Son of Man will be forgiven. But he who slanders the Holy Spirit will not be forgiven.

"When they bring you before synagogs, rulers, and authorities, don't worry how you will defend yourselves or what you will say. When that time comes, the Holy Spirit will teach you what to say."

Don't Be Greedy

"Teacher," someone in the crowd said to Him, "tell my brother to give me my share of the property our father left us."

"Man," He asked him, "who appointed Me to be your judge or to divide your property?

"Be careful," He told the people. "Guard against every

kind of greed. Even if you have more than enough, your property doesn't give you life."

Then He told them a story:

"A rich man had good crops on his land. 'What am I going to do?' he said to himself. 'I have no place to store my crops.' Finally he said, 'This is what I'll do: I'll tear down my barns and build bigger ones and store all my grain and goods in them. Then I'll say to myself, You have a lot of good things stored up for many years. Take life easy, eat, drink, and enjoy yourself.'

"But God said to him, 'You fool, tonight you die. And what you've prepared — who will get it?' That's how it is when you store up goods for yourself and aren't rich in God.

"That is why I tell you," He said to His disciples: "Don't worry about what you'll eat to keep alive or what you'll wear on your bodies. Life is more than food, and the body more than clothes. Look at the crows. They don't sow or cut grain, they have no storeroom or barn; and yet God feeds them. You're worth much more than birds. And can any of you by worrying add anything to your life? If you can't do even the smallest thing, why worry about the rest? See how the flowers grow. They don't work or spin. Yet I tell you, even Solomon in all his glory didn't dress like one of them. If that's how God dresses the grass, which lives in the field today and tomorrow is thrown into a stove, how much more certainly will He put clothes on you — who trust Him so little? So don't just think of what you'll eat or drink, and don't worry. The people in the world run after all these things, but your Father knows you need them. Only be eager to have Him as your King, and you'll get these things too. Don't be afraid, little flock. Your Father has decided to give you the kingdom.

"Sell what you have and give the money to the poor. Make yourselves purses that don't wear out and a treasure that will never be used up — in heaven, where no thief gets near it and no moth destroys it. Where your treasure is, there your heart will be."

Sorrow Ahead

"I have come to bring fire on earth, and how glad I would be if it were already started! I must be baptized with a baptism, and how I am troubled till it is done!

"Do you think I came to bring peace on earth? No, I tell you — to bring division. From now on five in one family will be divided, three against two and two against three. A father will be against a son and *a son against a father,* a mother against a daughter and *a daughter against her mother,* a mother-in-law against her daughter-in-law and *a daughter-in-law against her mother-in-law.*" [110]

This Is Your Opportunity

"When you see a cloud coming up in the west," Jesus said to the people, "you immediately say, 'There's going to be a heavy rain,' and so it rains. And when you see a wind blowing from the south, you say, 'It's going to be hot,' and so it is. You hypocrites! You can tell what the appearance of the earth and of the sky means. How is it that you can't interpret this present time? Why don't you yourselves decide what is right?

"When you go with your opponent to be tried before a ruler, do your best to settle with him on the way, or he may drag you before the judge, and the judge will hand you over to the officer, and the officer will put you in prison. I tell you, you will never get out till you pay the last cent."

Repent

At that time some men were there to tell Him about the Galileans whose blood Pilate had mixed with their sacrifices. Jesus asked them, "Do you think, because this happened to them, those Galileans must have been worse sinners than all the other Galileans? I tell you, no. And if you don't repent, you will all perish as they did. Or those eighteen the tower at Siloam fell on and killed — do you think they must have been worse transgressors than all the other people living in Jerusalem? I tell you, no. And if you don't repent, you will all perish as they did."

Another Year

He told them this story:

"A man had a fig tree growing in his vineyard. He came looking for fruit on it but didn't find any. So he said to the man who worked the vineyard, 'Look here! For the last three years I've come looking for figs on this fig tree and haven't found any. Cut it down. Why should it waste the ground?'

" 'Master,' he answered him, 'let it stand one more year, and I'll dig around it and fertilize it; it may have figs next year. If not, cut it down.' "

Crippled for 18 Years

Jesus was teaching in one of the synagogs on a Sabbath, and there was a woman whom a spirit had crippled for eighteen years. She was bent over and couldn't stand up straight. When Jesus saw her, He called her and said, "Woman, you're rid of your trouble." He laid His hands on her, and immediately she stood up straight and praised God.

But the synagog leader was annoyed with Jesus for healing on a Sabbath. "There are six days to do your work," he told the people. "Come on those days and get healed, but not on the day of rest."

"You hypocrites!" the Lord answered him. "Doesn't every one of you on a Saturday untie his ox or donkey from the manger and take it out to water? And this woman, a daughter of Abraham, whom the devil has bound these eighteen years, shouldn't she on the day of rest be freed from what bound her?"

As He said this, all His enemies had to feel ashamed, but all the common people were happy over the wonderful things He was doing.

"I and the Father Are One"

Then came the festival of Dedication in Jerusalem. It was winter, and Jesus was walking in Solomon's porch in the temple. There the Jews surrounded Him. "How long will You keep us in suspense?" they asked Him. "If You're the promised Savior, tell us frankly."

"I did tell you," Jesus answered them, "but you don't believe it. The works I do in My Father's name tell the truth about Me. But you don't believe, because you're not My sheep. My sheep listen to My voice, and I know them, and they follow Me, and I give them everlasting life. They will never be lost, and nobody will tear them out of My hand. My Father, who gave them to Me, is greater than all others, and nobody can tear them out of My Father's hand. I and the Father are one."

Again the Jews picked up stones to stone Him. Jesus answered them, "I have shown you many good works that come from the Father. For which of these works are you trying to stone Me?"

"We're stoning You," the Jews answered Him, "not for a good work but for blasphemy because You, a man, claim to be God."

Jesus said to them, "Isn't it written in your Bible, *I said, 'You are gods'?* [111] If it called them gods to whom God's Word came — and the Bible can't be set aside — do you say to Me, whom the Father appointed for His holy purpose and sent into the world, 'You're blaspheming,' because I said, 'I'm God's Son'? If I'm not doing My Father's works, don't trust Me. But if I do them, even if you don't trust Me, trust My works so as to learn and understand the Father is in Me and I am in the Father."

Again they tried to arrest Him, but He escaped from their hands. He went back across the Jordan to the place where John had been baptizing earlier, and He stayed there.

And again large crowds followed Him and gathered around Him, and He made them well there and taught them again as He used to do.

"John did no miracle," they said, "but everything John said about this One is true." And many believed in Him there.

·7·

In Perea

The Narrow Door

Then Jesus went and taught in one town and village after another on His way to Jerusalem.

Someone asked Him, "Lord, are only a few people saved?"

"Struggle to get in through the narrow door," He told them. "I tell you, many will try to get in and not succeed. After the Owner of the house gets up and closes the door, you'll be standing outside and knocking at the door. 'Lord, open up for us!' you'll say. But He'll answer you, 'I don't know where you're from.' Then you'll say, 'We ate and drank with You, and You taught in our streets.' But He'll tell you, 'I don't know where you're from. *Get away from Me, all you who do wrong.*' [112] Then you will cry and grind your teeth when you see Abraham, Isaac, Jacob, and all the prophets in God's kingdom but yourselves thrown out. People will come *from the east and the west,*[113] the north and the south, and will eat in God's kingdom. You see, some who are last will be first, and some who are first will be last."

Jesus Warns Jerusalem

Just then some Pharisees came and told Him, "Leave and get away from here; Herod wants to kill You."

"Go," He answered them, "and tell that fox, 'Listen, today and tomorrow I will drive out devils and do healings, and on the third day I will finish.' But I must be on My way today, tomorrow, and the next day, because a prophet just can't be killed outside Jerusalem.

"Jerusalem, Jerusalem, you murder the prophets and stone those sent to you! How often I wanted to gather your children the way a hen gathers her chicks under her wings, but you didn't want to! Look, now your *house is left*[114] to you. I tell you, you will not see Me till you say, '*Blessed is He who is coming in the Lord's name.*'"[115]

Dinner Is Ready!

Once on a Saturday Jesus went to the home of a leader of the Pharisees to eat a meal, and they were watching Him carefully.

In front of Him was a man who had dropsy. This led Jesus to ask the experts in the Law and the Pharisees, "Is it right to heal on a day of rest or not?" But they didn't say anything.

So Jesus took hold of the man, made him well, and sent him away. "If your son or your ox falls into a well," He asked them, "won't anyone of you pull him out immediately on a Sabbath?" They couldn't answer this.

He noticed how the guests were trying to get the places of honor, and so He used the scene to teach them: "When anyone invites you to a wedding, don't take the place of honor. He may have invited somebody more important than you. And he who invited you and him will come and tell you, 'Give this man your place,' and then you'll feel ashamed when you have to take the lowest place. No, when you're invited, go and take the lowest place, so that when your host comes he'll tell you, 'Friend, move up higher.' Then all your fellow guests will see how you're honored. If you honor yourself, you'll be humbled, but if you humble yourself, you'll be honored."

Then He told the man who had invited Him, "When you give a dinner or a supper, don't invite your friends, your brothers, your relatives, or rich neighbors. Otherwise they'll invite you too and pay you back. No, when you give a banquet, invite the poor, crippled, lame, and blind. Then you'll be happy because they can't pay you back. You'll be paid back when the righteous rise from the dead."

When one of those eating with Him heard this, he said to Jesus, "Happy is he who will eat bread in God's kingdom."

Jesus said to him:

"A man once gave a big dinner and invited many. When it was time for the dinner, he sent his slave to tell those who were invited, 'Come, it's ready now!'

"Then they all alike began to excuse themselves. 'I bought a field,' the first told him, 'and I've got to go out and see it. Please excuse me.' Another said, 'I bought five teams of oxen, and I'm on my way to try them out. Please excuse me.' And another said, 'I just got married, and that's why I can't come.'

"The slave went back and reported this to his master. Then the master of the house got angry. 'Go out quickly into the streets and alleys of the city,' he told his slave, 'and bring in here the poor, crippled, blind, and lame.'

"And the slave said, 'Master, it's done as you ordered, and there's still room.'

"Then the master told the slave, 'Go out to the roads and stone fences, and make them come in! I want my house to be full. I tell you, none of those men who were invited will taste my dinner.' "

Leave Everything

Large crowds were going with Jesus. Turning to them, He said, "If you come to Me and don't hate your father, mother, wife, children, brothers, and sisters and even your own life, you can't be My disciple. Whoever doesn't carry his cross and follow Me can't be My disciple.

"If anyone of you wants to build a tower, won't you first sit down and figure out what it costs, to see if you have enough to finish it? Otherwise, when you've laid a foundation but can't finish the building, all who watch you will make fun of you and say, 'This fellow started to build but couldn't finish it.'

"Or suppose a king is going into battle against another king. Won't he first sit down and consider if with ten thousand men he can oppose the other coming against him with twenty thousand? If he can't, then, while the other is still far away, he sends ambassadors to ask for terms of peace. Just so, anyone of you who doesn't say good-by to everything he has can't be My disciple.

"Now, salt is good. But if the salt loses its taste, how will it be made salty again? It is no good for the ground or for the manure pile. People throw it away.

"If you have ears to hear, listen!"

Lost—a Sheep

All the tax collectors and sinners were coming to Jesus to hear Him. But the Pharisees and the Bible scholars grumbled and said, "This Man welcomes sinners and eats with them."

So He told them this story:

"If anyone of you has a hundred sheep and loses one of them, don't you leave the ninety-nine in the wilderness and go after the lost one till you find it? When you find it, you lay it on your shoulders and are glad. You go home and call your friends and neighbors together and say to them, 'Be happy with me. I found my lost sheep!' So, I tell you, there will be more joy in heaven over one sinner who repents than over ninety-nine good people who don't need to repent."

Lost—a Coin

"Or suppose a woman has ten coins and loses one. Won't she light a lamp and sweep the house and look for it carefully till she finds it? When she finds it, she calls her women friends and neighbors together and says, 'Be happy with me. I found the coin I lost.' So, I tell you, God's angels will be happy over one sinner who repents."

Lost—a Son

Then Jesus said: "A man had two sons. The younger of them said to his father, 'Father, give me my share of the property.' So he divided his property between them.

"A few days later the younger son cashed in all he had, left home for a distant country, and there squandered his property by wild living. When he had spent it all, a bad famine came over that country, and he started to be in need. So he went and hired himself out to a citizen of that country, who sent him to his fields to feed hogs. And he would have been glad to fill up on the pods the hogs were eating. And nobody would give him anything.

"Then he came to his senses and said, 'How many of my father's hired men have more food than they can eat, and here I'm starving to death. I'll start out and go to my father and tell him, "Father, I've sinned against heaven and against you. I don't deserve to be called your son anymore. Make me one of your hired men." '

"So he started out and went to his father. While he was still far away, his father saw him and felt sorry for him. He ran and put his arms around him and kissed him. 'Father,' the son told him, 'I've sinned against heaven and against you.

I don't deserve to be called your son anymore. Make me one of your hired men.'

" 'Quick,' the father told his slaves, 'bring out a robe — the best — and put it on him, put a ring on his finger and shoes on his feet. And bring the fattened calf, kill it, and let's eat and celebrate. This son of mine was dead and is alive. He was lost and is found.' And they started to celebrate.

"Now, his older son was out in the field. As he was coming in, he got near the house — he heard music and dancing! Calling one of the servants, he asked, 'What's going on here?'

" 'Your brother's home,' he was told, 'and your father has killed the fattened calf because he got him back safe and sound.'

"Then he got angry and wouldn't go in. So his father came out and begged him. But he answered his father, 'All these years I've been working like a slave for you and have never disobeyed your order, and you never gave me even a little goat to celebrate with my friends. But as soon as this son of yours came back, who devoured your property with prostitutes, you killed the fattened calf for him.'

" 'Son,' the father said to him, 'you're always with me, and everything I have is yours. But we had to celebrate and be glad. This brother of yours was dead and is alive. He was lost and is found.' "

The Dishonest Manager

Then Jesus said to His disciples:

"There was a rich man whose manager was accused of squandering the man's property. He called the manager. 'What's this I hear about you?' he asked him. 'Give an account of your management, because you can't manage my property any longer.'

" 'What'll I do?' the manager said to himself. 'My master is taking my job away from me. I'm not strong enough to dig;

I'm ashamed to beg. I know what I'll do so that when I've lost my job people will welcome me into their homes.'

"So he called everyone who owed his master anything. 'How much do you owe my master?' he asked the first.

" 'Eight hundred gallons of oil,' he answered.

" 'Take your note,' he said, 'sit down quick and write "four hundred." '

"Then he asked another, 'How much do you owe?'

" 'A thousand bushels of wheat,' he answered.

" 'Take your note,' he told him, 'and write "eight hundred." '

"And the master praised the dishonest manager for acting so shrewdly.

"In dealing with their own kind of people the men of this world are shrewder than those who are in the light.

"And I tell you, with the money that's often used in wrong ways win friends for yourselves so that when it's gone you'll be welcomed into the everlasting homes. If you can be trusted with very little, you can be trusted with much. And if you're dishonest with very little, you're dishonest with much. If you couldn't be trusted with wicked money, who will trust you with that which is really good? And if you couldn't be trusted with someone else's things, who will give you your own?

"No servant can be the slave of two masters. Either he will hate the one and love the other, or he'll be loyal to the one and despise the other. You can't serve God and money."

The money-loving Pharisees heard all this and turned up their noses at Him. Then He said to them, "You try to make people think you're good, but God knows your hearts. What people consider great is detested by God.

"The Law and the prophets were until John. Since then the good news of God's kingdom is told, and everybody tries to force his way into it. It is easier for heaven and earth to disappear than for the Law to drop one dot of an *i*."

Husband and Wife

Some Pharisees, coming to Him to test Him, asked Him, "Is it right for a man to divorce his wife for any reason?"

"What did Moses order you to do?" He asked them.

"Moses let a man *make out a divorce paper and divorce his wife*," [116] they said.

"He wrote this law for you on account of your closed minds," Jesus told them, "and let you divorce your wives, but originally there was no such thing. Haven't you read that when God made the world He who created them from the beginning *made them a male and a female?*" [117] And He added: "*That is why a man will leave his father and mother and live with his wife, and the two will be one flesh.*[118] And so they are no more two but one flesh. Now, what God has joined together man must not separate."

In the house the disciples also asked Him about this. "I tell you," He answered them, "if anyone divorces his wife, except for adultery, and marries another, he's living in adultery with her. And if a wife divorces her husband and marries another man, she's living in adultery. And the man who marries a woman divorced from her husband is living in adultery."

"If a man has to have such grounds in dealing with his wife," the disciples told Him, "it's better not to marry."

"Not all can do this," He told them, "only those to whom it has been given. Some can't marry because they were born that way. Others, because they have been mutilated by men. And still others have decided to do without marriage for the kingdom of heaven. If anyone can do it, let him do it."

The Rich Man and Lazarus

"There was a rich man who used to dress in purple and fine linen and live in luxury every day. A beggar by the name of Lazarus was laid at his gate. He was covered with sores and longed to satisfy his hunger with anything that might fall from the rich man's table. And the dogs would even come and lick his sores.

"One day the beggar died, and the angels carried him to Abraham's bosom. The rich man also died and was buried. Being tormented in hell, he looked up, and though far away, he saw Abraham, and Lazarus at his bosom. 'Father Abraham,' he called, 'have pity on me and send Lazarus to dip the tip of his finger in water and cool off my tongue, because I'm suffering in this fire.'

"But Abraham said, 'Remember, son, you had your good things in your life, while Lazarus had his misery. Now he is comforted here, while you're suffering. In all these things there's a wide chasm fixed between us and you, so that those who might want to cross from here over to you can't do it, nor do any from there come over to us.'

"'Then I ask you, father,' he said, 'send him to my father's home — I have five brothers — to warn them not to get into this place of torture.'

"'They have Moses and the prophets,' Abraham said. 'They should listen to them.'

"'No, Father Abraham,' he said, 'but if someone comes to them from the dead, they'll repent.'

"'If they don't listen to Moses and the prophets,' he answered him, 'they won't be convinced even if somebody rose from the dead.'"

Faith and Duty

Then the apostles said to the Lord, "Give us more faith."

"If you have a faith like a mustard seed," the Lord said, "you could say to this mulberry tree, 'Be pulled up by the roots, and be planted in the lake,' and it would obey you.

"If your slave is plowing or watching sheep and comes in from the field, will any of you say to him, 'Come quickly and eat'? Or won't you rather tell him, 'Prepare something for me to eat, fasten your belt, and serve me while I eat and drink, and afterwards you eat and drink'? You won't thank the slave for doing what he was ordered to do, will you? So you too, when you've done all you were ordered to do, say, 'We are slaves who claim no credit. We've only done our duty.' "

· 8 ·

On the Way to Jerusalem

Jesus Raises Lazarus

Then Lazarus was sick. He was in Bethany, the village where Mary and her sister Martha were living. Mary was the one who poured perfume on the Lord and wiped His feet with her hair. It was her brother Lazarus who was sick.

So the sisters sent someone to tell Jesus, "Lord, the one You love is sick."

When Jesus heard it, He said, "The purpose of this sickness isn't death but to show God's glory; it is to glorify God's Son."

Jesus loved Martha and her sister and Lazarus. Now, when He heard Lazarus was sick, He stayed two days where He was. After that He said to His disciples, "Let us go back to Judea."

"Master," the disciples said to Him, "the Jews have just been wanting to stone You, and You're going back there?"

"Aren't there twelve hours in a day?" Jesus answered. "If you walk during the day, you don't stumble, because you see the light of this world. But if you walk at night, you stumble, because you have no light."

After He said this, He told them, "Our friend Lazarus has gone to sleep, but I'm going there to wake him up."

"Lord, if he has gone to sleep," His disciples said to Him, "he'll get well."

Jesus meant he was dead, but they thought He meant he was only sleeping. Then Jesus told them in plain words, "Lazarus died. And I'm glad I wasn't there; it will help you believe. But let us go to him."

Then Thomas, who was called Twin, said to his fellow disciples, "Let us go too and die with Him."

When Jesus got there, He found that Lazarus had been in the grave four days already.

Bethany was near Jerusalem, not quite two miles away, and many Jews had come to Martha and Mary to comfort them about their brother.

Now, when Martha heard, "Jesus is coming," she went to meet Him, while Mary stayed at home. "Lord, if You had been here," Martha told Jesus, "my brother wouldn't have died. But even now I know God will give You anything You ask Him."

"Your brother will rise again," Jesus told her.

"I know he'll rise again," Martha answered Him, "in the resurrection on the last day."

"I am the Resurrection and the Life," Jesus said to her. "Anyone who believes in Me will live even if he dies. Yes, anyone who lives and believes in Me will never die. Do you believe that?"

"Yes, Lord," she told Him, "I believe You are the promised Savior, God's Son, who is coming into the world."

After she said this, she went to call her sister Mary. "The Teacher is here," she whispered, "and is calling for you."

When Mary heard it, she got up quickly to go to Him.

Jesus hadn't come to the village yet but was still where Martha had met Him. Now, the Jews who were in the house with Mary to comfort her saw her get up quickly and leave. So they followed her, thinking she was going to the grave to weep there. When Mary came where Jesus was and saw Him, she bowed down at His feet and said, "Lord, if You had been here, my brother wouldn't have died."

When Jesus saw her weeping, and the Jews weeping who came with her, He groaned deeply and was troubled.

"Where did you lay him?" He asked.

"Lord, come and see," they answered Him.

Jesus burst into tears. "See how He loved him," the Jews said. But some of them asked, "He gave sight to the blind man — couldn't He have kept this man from dying?"

Groaning deeply again, Jesus went to the grave. It was a cave, and a stone was laid against it. "Move the stone away," said Jesus.

Martha, the dead man's sister, told Him, "Lord, he smells already. He's been dead four days."

Jesus said to her, "Didn't I tell you, 'If you believe, you will see God's glory'?" So they moved the stone away.

Jesus looked up and said, "Father, I thank You for hearing Me. I knew You always hear Me. But I spoke so that the people standing around Me will believe You sent Me." After He had said this, He called out loud, "Lazarus, come out!"

The dead man came out, his feet and hands wrapped in bandages and his face wrapped in a cloth. "Unwrap him," Jesus told them, "and let him go."

Then many of the Jews who had come to Mary and had seen what He did believed in Him. But some of them went to the Pharisees and told them what Jesus had done. Then the ruling priests and the Pharisees called a meeting of the council. "What are we doing?" they asked. "This Man is doing many miracles. If we let Him go on like this, everybody will believe in Him, and then the Romans will come and take away our place and our nation."

But one of them, Caiaphas, who was high priest that year, told them, "You don't know anything, and you don't consider it is better for you that one man dies instead of the people and the whole nation doesn't perish." He didn't think of this himself, but being high priest that year, he prophesied Jesus was going to die for the nation and not only for this nation but also to bring God's scattered children together and make them one.

From that day on they planned to kill Him. So Jesus no longer walked in public among the Jews but left and went into the country near the wilderness, to a town called Ephraim and stayed there with His disciples.

Only One Thanks God

On His way to Jerusalem, Jesus traveled along the border between Samaria and Galilee. As He came to a village, ten lepers came toward Him. They stopped at a distance and called out, "Jesus, Master, have pity on us!"

When He saw them, He told them, "Go and *let the priests examine* [119] you."

And here's what happened: As they went, they were cleansed of their leprosy. One of them, seeing he was healed, turned back and loudly praised God. He bowed to the ground at Jesus' feet and thanked Him. And he was a Samaritan.

"Weren't there ten cleansed?" Jesus asked. "But the nine — where are they? Weren't there any who came back to give God glory except this foreigner?"

And He told him, "Get up and go! Your faith made you well."

Where Is God's Kingdom?

"When will God's kingdom come?" the Pharisees asked Jesus.

"People can't see the coming of God's kingdom," He

answered them. "They will not say, 'Look, here it is!' or, 'There it is!' You see, God's kingdom is now among you."

God Hears

Jesus told them a story to show that they should always pray and not get tired of it:

"In a town there was a judge who didn't fear God or care what people thought. In that town there was also a widow who kept coming to him and saying, 'Get me justice and defend me against my enemy!'

"For a while he refused to do anything, but then he said to himself, 'Even though I don't fear God or care what people think, yet because this widow keeps bothering me, I'll have to see that she gets justice, or she'll keep coming till she wears me out.'"

The Lord added, "Listen to what the unjust judge says. And won't God get justice for His chosen ones who cry to Him day and night? Is He slow to help them? I tell you, He will quickly get justice for them. But when the Son of Man comes, will He find faith on earth?"

The Pharisee and the Tax Collector

Jesus told this story to some who were sure they were righteous and so looked down on everybody else:

"Two men went up to the temple to pray. One was a Pharisee and the other a tax collector. The Pharisee stood and prayed by himself: 'God, I thank You I'm not like the other people: robbers, wrongdoers, adulterers, or even like that tax collector. I fast twice a week and give a tenth of all my income.'

"But the tax collector, standing a distance away, wouldn't even look up to heaven but was beating his breast and saying, 'God, forgive me, a sinner!'

"I tell you, this man, and not the other, went home righteous. Everyone who honors himself will be humbled; but if you humble yourself, you will be honored."

Jesus Loves Children

Then some people brought babies to Jesus to have Him lay His hands on them and pray. When the disciples saw them, they sternly told them not to do it.

But when Jesus saw this, He didn't like it at all. He called the children to Him and said, "Let the little children come to Me, and don't keep them away. God's kingdom belongs to such as these. I tell you the truth, if you don't receive God's kingdom like a little child, you will not get into it."

He took them in His arms, laid His hands on them and blessed them, and then went away.

The Rich Young Leader

As Jesus was coming out to the road, an official came running to Him and knelt before Him. "Good Teacher," he asked Him, "what good thing should I do to get everlasting life?"

"Why do you call Me good?" Jesus asked him. "Nobody is good except One — God. Why do you ask Me about something good? If you want to go into life, keep the commandments."

"Which commandments?" he asked Him.

"You know the commandments," Jesus said. *"Don't murder, don't commit adultery, don't steal, don't lie,* don't rob, *honor your father and mother,*[120] and *love your neighbor like yourself."* [121]

"Teacher," the young man told Him, "I've kept all these since I was a child. What else do I need?"

When Jesus heard this, He looked at him and loved him. "You still lack one thing," He told him. "If you want to be perfect, go, sell everything you have, distribute the money among the poor, and you'll have a treasure in heaven. Then come and follow Me."

When the young man heard this, he looked gloomy and went away very sad, because he was very rich. Jesus watched him and then looked around. "I tell you the truth," He said to His disciples, "it is hard for rich people to get into God's kingdom!"

The disciples were surprised that He said that. But Jesus said to them again, "Children, how hard it is to get into God's kingdom! Again I tell you it's easier for a camel to go through a needle's eye than for a rich man to get into God's kingdom."

The disciples, hearing this, were dumfounded. "Who, then, can be saved?" they asked one another.

"Men can't do this," Jesus said as He looked at them. "But God can, because *God can do anything.*" [122]

Then Peter spoke up: "Look! We gave up everything and followed You. So what will we get?"

"Let Me assure you," Jesus said to them, "in the new life, when the Son of Man sits on His throne of glory, you who followed Me will also sit on twelve thrones and rule the twelve tribes of Israel. And everyone who gave up his home or wife, brothers or sisters, mother, father, or children, or fields for Me and for the good news — for God's kingdom — will certainly get a hundred times as much here in this life: houses, brothers and sisters, mothers and children and fields, with persecutions, and in the coming world everlasting life. But many who are first will be last, and many who are last will be first."

"The Last Will Be First"

"The kingdom of heaven is like the owner of a place who went out early in the morning to hire men to work in his vineyard. He agreed with the workers to pay them a denarius a day and sent them into his vineyard. About nine o'clock he went out and saw others standing in the marketplace doing nothing. 'You go into the vineyard too,' he told them, 'and I'll pay you what's right.' So they went.

"He went out again about twelve o'clock and three

o'clock and did the same thing. About five o'clock he went out and found some others standing around. 'Why are you standing here all day long doing nothing?' he asked them.

" 'Nobody has hired us,' they answered him.

" 'You go into the vineyard too,' he told them.

"When evening came, the owner of the vineyard told his manager, 'Call the men and give them their pay. Start with the last and go on to the first.'

"Those who started working around five o'clock came, and each got a denarius. When the first ones came, they expected to get more, but each of them too got a denarius. They took it, but they grumbled against the owner: 'These last men worked only one hour, and you've treated them exactly like us who have worked hard all day in the blazing sun.'

" 'Friend, I'm doing you no wrong,' he answered one of them. 'You agreed with me on a denarius, didn't you? Take your money and go. I want to give this last man as much as I give you. Don't I have the right to do as I please with what is mine? Or are you jealous because I'm generous?'

"In this way the last will be first and the first last."

"I Will Die and Rise Again"

As they were on their way up to Jerusalem, Jesus walked ahead of them. They were amazed, and the others who were following Him were afraid. So once again He took the twelve by themselves and on the way told them what was going to happen to Him:

"Look, we're going up to Jerusalem, and everything the prophets wrote for the Son of Man will be done: The Son of Man will be betrayed to the ruling priests and the Bible scholars, who will condemn Him to die and hand Him over to the non-Jews. They'll mock and insult Him, spit on Him, scourge Him, crucify and kill Him. But on the third day He will rise."

But they understood none of this. It was a mystery to them, and they didn't know what He meant.

The Cup of Suffering

Then the mother of James and John, Zebedee's sons, came to Jesus with her sons and bowed before Him to ask Him for something. "Teacher," they said to Him, "we want You to do for us what we ask."

"What do you want Me to do for you?" He asked them.

She told Him, "Promise that one of my two sons will sit at Your right and the other at Your left in Your kingdom of glory."

"You don't know what you're asking," Jesus answered them. "Can you drink the cup I'm going to drink or be baptized with the baptism with which I'm being baptized?"

"We can," they told Him.

"You'll drink the cup I'm drinking," Jesus told them, "and be baptized with the baptism with which I'm being baptized. But sitting at My right and left is something I can give only to those for whom My Father prepared it."

When the other ten heard about it, they got angry with James and John. Then Jesus called them and told them, "You know that those who are considered rulers of the nations are lords over them, and their great men are tyrants over them. But among you it's different. Anyone who wants to become great among you will have to serve you, and anyone who wants to be first among you will have to be everybody's slave. Why, even the Son of Man didn't come to be served but to serve and give His life as a ransom for all people."

Two Blind Men

Then they came to Jericho. As Jesus and His disciples and many people were leaving Jericho, a large crowd followed Him. And there were two blind men sitting by the road. One was Bartimaeus, the son of Timaeus, a blind beggar. Hearing a crowd go by, he tried to find out what it was all about. "Jesus from Nazareth is passing by," they told him.

When they heard, "Jesus is passing by," they called, "Jesus, Lord, have pity on us, Son of David!"

The crowd urged them to be quiet. But they called all the louder, "Lord, have pity on us, Son of David!"

Jesus stopped and said, "Call them." They called the blind men and told them, "Cheer up! Get up! He's calling you." They laid aside their garments, jumped up, and went to Jesus.

"What do you want Me to do for you?" Jesus asked.

"Lord, we want to see," they told Him.

Jesus felt sorry for them and touched their eyes. "See!" Jesus told them. "Go! Your faith has made you well."

And immediately they could see. And they followed Him on the road, praising God. And all the people praised God for what they had seen.

Zacchaeus

He went into Jericho and was passing through it. Here there was a man by the name of Zacchaeus. He was an overseer of tax collectors and was rich. He was trying to see what kind of person Jesus was, but being a small man, he couldn't see Him on account of the crowd. So he ran ahead and climbed up a fig-mulberry tree to see Him, because Jesus was coming that way.

When Jesus came to the place, He looked up. "Zacchaeus, hurry down," He told him. "Today I must stay at your home."

He hurried down and was happy to welcome Him. But all who saw them started to grumble: "He went to be the guest of a sinful man."

Zacchaeus stood there and said to the Lord, "Look, Lord, half of my property I'm giving to the poor, and if I've cheated anybody, I'm paying him back four times as much."

"Today salvation has come to this home," Jesus told him, "since he too is a son of Abraham. The Son of Man came to *look for* and save *the lost*." [123]

Use God's Gifts

While they were listening to this, Jesus went on to tell them a story, because He was near Jerusalem and they thought God's kingdom was to appear immediately.

"A nobleman," He said, "went to a distant country to be made a king and then come back. He called ten of his slaves, gave them a thousand denarii,* and told them, 'Trade with these till I come.'

"But the men of his own country hated him and sent representatives after him to say, 'We don't want this man to be our king.'

"But he was made king. When he came back, he said, 'Call those slaves whom I gave the money. I want to see what each one has made by his trading.'

"The first came and said, 'Master, your hundred denarii have made a thousand more denarii.'

" 'Well done, my good slave!' he told him. 'You proved you could be trusted in a very small matter. Take charge of ten cities.'

"The second came and said, 'Your hundred denarii, master, made five hundred denarii.'

" 'You be in charge of five cities,' he told this one.

"Then the one who was different came and said, 'Master, here are your hundred denarii. I put them away in a cloth and kept them there. I was afraid of you. You're a hard man. You take what you didn't deposit, and you get grain you didn't sow.'

" 'I'll judge you by what you say, you wicked slave!' he told him. 'You knew I'm a hard man, taking what I didn't deposit and getting grain I didn't sow? Why didn't you put my money in the bank? Then, when I came back, I could have collected it with interest.' So he told his men, 'Take his hundred denarii away and give them to the man who has a thousand.'

* One denarius was a day's pay.

" 'Master,' they answered him, 'he has a thousand denarii.'

" 'I tell you, everyone who has something will be given more, and anyone who doesn't have what he should have, even what he has will be taken away. But those enemies of mine who didn't want me to be their king — bring them here and kill them in front of me.' "

After Jesus had said this, He continued on His way up to Jerusalem.

Mary Anoints Jesus

The Jewish Passover was near, and many came from the country to Jerusalem before the Passover to purify themselves. They were looking for Jesus and asking one another as they stood in the temple, "What do you think? He isn't coming to the festival, is He?" The ruling priests and the Pharisees had given orders if anyone found out where He was he should report it so that they might arrest Him.

Six days before the Passover, Jesus came to Bethany, where Lazarus was, whom Jesus had raised from the dead. He went into the home of Simon the leper. There a dinner was prepared for Him. Martha served, and Lazarus was one of those eating with Him.

Then Mary took a pound of perfume, real nard and very expensive, in an alabaster jar, and she came to Him while He was lying at the table, broke the jar, and poured the perfume on Jesus' head and feet and dried His feet with her hair. The fragrance of the perfume filled the house.

The disciples saw it and didn't like it. Some who were there felt annoyed and said to one another, "Why was the perfume wasted like this?" And they were grumbling at her.

Judas (the man from Kerioth, one of His disciples, who was going to betray Him) asked, "Why wasn't this perfume sold for three hundred denarii and the money given to the poor?" He didn't say this because he cared about the poor but because he was a thief and used to steal what was put in the money box he carried.

Knowing what was going on, Jesus said to them, "Let her alone. Why should you trouble her? She has done a beautiful thing to Me. The poor you always have with you, and you can help them whenever you want to, but you will not always have Me. She has done what she could. She came ahead of time to pour this perfume on My body to prepare Me for My burial. I tell you, wherever this good news is preached in the whole world, certainly what she has done will also be told in memory of her."

A large crowd of the Jews found out He was there, and they came not only on account of Jesus but also to see Lazarus, whom He had raised from the dead. But the ruling priests decided to kill Lazarus too, because he was the reason many Jews were going over to Jesus and believing in Him.

(Some of the material found near the Dead Sea suggests the possibility of a different dating for what happened from the Saturday before Palm Sunday to Good Friday. But the dating used here fits the text of our Gospels best.)

· 9

In Jerusalem

The King Is Coming

The next day, when they were getting near Jerusalem and came to Bethphage and Bethany, at the Mount of Olives, Jesus sent two of His disciples. "Go into the village ahead of you," He told them, "and just as you go in, you'll find a donkey tied up and a colt tied with her that nobody ever sat on. Untie them and bring them to Me. And if anybody asks you, 'Why are you doing that?' say, 'The Lord needs it and will promptly send it back here.' And immediately he will send them."

The disciples whom He sent went and did as Jesus had directed them. They found the colt tied to the gate, outside in the street, as He had told them.

While they were untying the colt, its owners, who were standing there, asked them, "What are you doing, untying the colt?"

"The Lord needs it," they said. And the men let them go.

So they brought the donkey and the colt to Jesus, put their garments on them, and set Jesus on the colt.

The people who had been with Him when He called Lazarus out of the grave and raised him from the dead were telling what they had seen. When the large crowd that had come to the festival heard He had done this miracle and heard, "Jesus is coming to Jerusalem," they took branches from the palm trees and went out to meet Him. As He was riding along, most of the people spread their garments on the road, and others spread leafy branches that they cut from the trees in the fields and spread them on the road.

This happened so that what the prophet said would come true:

Tell the daughter of Zion, "Don't be afraid!
Look! Your King is coming to you,
Gentle, riding on a donkey and on a colt of a donkey." [124]

At that time His disciples didn't know what it meant, but after Jesus was glorified, they remembered this was written about Him and was done to Him.

"Stop Them"

As He was coming near the place where the road goes down the Mount of Olives, the whole crowd of the disciples, who went ahead of Him and followed Him, began to praise God joyfully and loudly for all the miracles they had seen. They were shouting:

"Our Savior, the Son of David!
Blessed is He who is coming in the Lord's name! [125]
The King of Israel!
Blessed is the coming kingdom of our father David!
In heaven peace, and glory in the highest heavens."

Then the Pharisees said to one another, "You see, you're not getting anywhere. Look! The world is running after Him."

Some of the Pharisees in the crowd said to Him, "Teacher, urge Your disciples to be quiet."

"I tell you," He answered them, "if these are quiet, the stones will cry out."

When He came near and saw the city, He wept loud over it and said, "If today you only knew — yes, you — the way to peace! But now it's hidden so that you can't see it. The time will come for you when your enemies will put up ramparts against you and surround you and press against you from every side. They'll *dash* you and *your children* to the *ground* [126] and not leave one stone on another in you, because you didn't know the time your help came to you."

When He came into Jerusalem, the whole city was excited, asking, "Who is this?"

The crowds answered, "This is the Prophet Jesus from Nazareth in Galilee."

He came into the temple and looked around at everything. Blind and lame persons came to Him in the temple, and He made them well.

When the ruling priests and the Bible scholars saw the wonderful things He did, and the children shouting in the temple, "*Our Savior,* [125] the Son of David!" they didn't like it at all. "Do You hear what they're saying?" they asked Him.

"Yes," Jesus answered them. "Haven't you ever read, *You have made children and babies at the breast praise You?*" [127]

Since it was late now, He left them and went with the twelve out of the city to Bethany and spent the night there.

Nothing but Leaves

The next day, in the morning, when they left Bethany to go back to the city, Jesus was hungry. In the distance, by the road, He saw a fig tree with leaves, and He went to see if He could find anything on it. When He came to it, He found nothing but leaves, because it wasn't the season for figs. Then He said to the tree, and His disciples heard Him: "May nobody ever eat fruit from you again!" And immediately the fig tree dried up.

He Cleans the Temple Again

When they came to Jerusalem, He went into the temple and proceeded to drive out all who were selling and buying in the temple and upset the tables of the money changers and the chairs of those who sold pigeons. He would not let anyone carry a vessel across the temple grounds.

Then He taught: "Isn't it written, *My house should be called a house of prayer for all the nations?* [128] But you made it *a den of robbers.*" [129]

Every day He was teaching in the temple. When the ruling priests, the Bible scholars, and the leaders of the people heard Him, they tried to find a way to kill Him. But they couldn't find a way to do it; they were afraid of Him, because He amazed all the people by His teaching and they were all eager to hear Him.

During the day He would teach in the temple, and when evening came, He would leave the city and go out to the Mount of Olives, as it was called, and stay there for the night. All the people used to get up early to go to Him in the temple and hear Him.

The Fig Tree Withers

When they walked by early in the morning, they saw the fig tree withered from the roots up. The disciples were surprised to see this. Peter, remembering, said to Him, "Master, look! The fig tree You cursed is dried up."

"How did the fig tree dry up so quickly?" they asked.

"Believe in God!" Jesus answered them. "I tell you the truth: If you believe and don't doubt, you will not only do what I did to the fig tree, but if you will say to this mount,*

* The Mount of Olives.

'Be lifted up and be thrown into the sea,' * and have no doubt in your mind but believe what you say will be done, it will be done for you. That's why I tell you, anything you ask for in prayer, believe that you received it, and you will have it. When you stand and pray, if you have anything against anyone, forgive him, so that your Father in heaven will forgive you your sins."

From Heaven

They came again to the temple in Jeusalem. As He was walking in the temple, teaching the people and telling them the good news, the ruling priests, the Bible scholars, and the elders of the people came to Him. "Tell us," they asked Him, "by what authority are You doing these things? Or who gave You the right to do them?"

Jesus answered them, "I will ask you a question. And if you answer Me, I'll tell you by what authority I'm doing these things. Tell Me, John's baptism — was it from heaven or from men? Answer Me."

They argued among themselves, "If we say, 'From heaven,' He will ask us, 'Then why didn't you believe him?' But if we say, 'From men,' we're afraid of the people. All the people will stone us. They're convinced John was a prophet." So they answered Jesus, "We don't know."

Then Jesus told them, "Neither will I tell you by what authority I'm doing these things."

Say and Do

"Now, what do you think of this? A man had two sons. He went to the first and said, 'Son, go and work in the vineyard today.'

" 'I won't,' he answered. Later he changed his mind and went.

* The Dead Sea, which can be seen from the Mount of Olives.

"The father went to the other one and told him the same thing. He answered, 'I will, sir,' but didn't go.

"Which of the two did what the father wanted?"

They answered, "The first."

Jesus said to them, "I tell you the truth, tax collectors and prostitutes are going into God's kingdom ahead of you. John came to you in a righteous way, but you didn't believe him; the tax collectors and prostitutes believed him. But even when you had seen that, you didn't change your minds and believe him."

God's Vineyard

Then He used stories in talking to the people:

"Listen to another story:

"A man who owned property *planted a vineyard. He put a wall around it, cut a winepress and a vat into the rock, and built a watchtower.*[130] Then he rented it out to workers and left home to be gone a long time.

"When the grapes were getting ripe, he sent a slave to the workers to get from them his share of the products of the vineyard. But the workers took him, beat him, and sent him back empty-handed. He sent another slave to them. They hit him on the head, treated him shamefully, and sent him back empty-handed. Then he sent a third slave. They stoned him, wounding him, and threw him out. He sent another, and that one they killed. Then he sent many other slaves, this time a larger number, and they treated these the same way. Some they beat, and others they killed.

"The owner of the vineyard had one more, a son, whom he loved. Finally he said, 'What should I do? I'll send my son whom I love. Maybe they'll respect my son.' So he sent his son to them.

"When those workers saw the son, they talked it over among themselves, saying, 'This is the heir. Come, let's kill him, and then we'll get the inheritance.' So they took him, threw him out of the vineyard, and killed him.

"Now, when the owner of the vineyard comes, what will he do to those workers?"

He was told, "He will have those scoundrels die a miserable death and rent out the vineyard to other workers who will bring him the grapes when they're ripe."

"That must never happen!" said those who heard Him.

Jesus looked at them and asked, "Haven't you ever read in your Bible, *The stone the builders rejected has become the cornerstone. The Lord has done it, and we think it is wonderful?* [131] That is why I tell you, God's kingdom will be taken away from you and be given to a people who will do its works. Everyone who falls on that Stone will be dashed in pieces, and if that Stone falls on anyone, It will scatter him like dust."

When the ruling priests and Pharisees and Bible scholars heard His stories, they knew He was talking about them. They wanted to grab Him then and there, because they knew He had aimed this story at them, but they were afraid because the people thought He was a prophet. So they let Him alone and went away.

Come to the Wedding!

Again Jesus used stories in talking to them. He said:

"The kingdom of heaven is like a king who prepared a wedding for his son. He sent his slaves to call those who had been invited to the wedding, but they refused to come. Then he sent other slaves and said to them, 'Tell the people who are invited, "Look here! I prepared my dinner. My bulls and fattened calves are killed, and everything is ready. Come to the wedding." '

"But they paid no attention and went away, one to his farm, another to his business, and the rest took his slaves, shamefully mistreated them, and murdered them.

"The king got angry. He sent his soldiers, and they killed those murderers and burned their city.

"Then he said to his slaves: 'The wedding is ready, but the people who were invited didn't deserve the honor. Now go where the roads leave the city, and call everybody you find there to the wedding.' Those slaves went out on the roads and brought in all the people they found, bad and good. And the wedding hall was filled with guests.

"When the king came in to look at the guests, he saw there a man without a wedding garment. 'Friend,' he asked him, 'how did you get in here without a wedding garment?'

"The man couldn't say a thing. Then the king told the servants, 'Tie him hand and foot, and throw him out into the dark. There he will cry and grind his teeth.'

"Many are invited, but few are chosen."

Taxes

Then the Pharisees went and plotted to trap Him with a question. They watched for an opportunity and sent their disciples with some of Herod's men to Him as spies to act holy in order to catch Him in what He would say. They wanted to hand Him over to the governor's control and authority.

When they came to Him, they said, "Teacher, we know You're honest. You're right in what You say and teach, and You don't care what others think, because You don't favor any special persons but really teach God's way. Now tell us: What do You think? Is it right for us to pay a tax to Caesar or not? Should we pay it or not?"

Seeing through their wicked and hypocritical way, Jesus asked them, "Why do you test Me, you hypocrites? Show Me the coin with which the tax is paid. Bring Me a denarius; I want to see it."

They brought Him a denarius. "Whose head is this and whose inscription?" He asked them.

"Caesar's," they told Him.

"Well, then, give Caesar what is Caesar's," He told them, "and God what is God's."

So they couldn't catch Him before the people in anything He said. His answer surprised them so much they didn't say anything. Then they let Him alone and went away.

The Dead Live

On that day some Sadducees, who say the dead don't rise, came to Him with this question: "Teacher, Moses wrote for us, *If anyone dies and leaves* a wife but *no child, his brother should marry his widow and have children for his brother.*[132] Now, there were seven brothers among us. The first married and died, and since he had no children, he left his widow to his brother. The second married her, died, and left no children. And so did the third. In the same way all seven died and left no children. Last of all the woman died too. Now, when they rise from the dead, which of the seven will be her husband? You know, all seven had her as wife."

"You're wrong," Jesus answered them. "You don't know your Bible or God's power. In this world men and women marry, but those who are considered worthy to rise from the dead and live in the other world don't marry but are like angels in heaven. Nor can they die anymore, because they're God's children and share in the resurrection. Moses showed that the dead rise. Didn't you read in the book of Moses, in the story of the bush, what God told you about the dead rising, how God told him, *I am the God of Abraham, the God of Isaac, and the God of Jacob?* [133] He's not the God of the dead but of the living. All who are with Him are alive. You're badly mistaken!"

His teaching amazed the people who heard Him.

Love God and Your Neighbor

When the Pharisees heard He had silenced the Sadducees, they got together. One of them, an expert in the Law, hearing the others argue with Him and seeing how well Jesus answered them, came to Him and tested Him by asking Him, "Teacher, which is the most important and greatest of all the commandments in the Law?"

Jesus answered, "The most important is: *Listen, Israel, the Lord our God alone is Lord. Then love the Lord your God with all your heart, with all your life,* with all your mind, *and with all your strength.*[134] This is the greatest and most important commandment. The next is like it: *Love your neighbor like yourself.*[135] No other commandment is greater than these. All the Law and the prophets depend on these two commandments."

"Right, Teacher!" the Bible scholar said to Him. "You told the truth: *He is the only One, and there is no other beside Him,* and *loving Him with all your heart,* with all your understanding, *and with all your strength,*[136] and *loving your neighbor like yourself* [135] is more than all the *burnt offerings and sacrifices.*" [137]

When Jesus saw how sensibly he answered, He told him, "You're not far from God's kingdom."

After that nobody dared to ask Him another question.

David's Son

While Jesus was teaching in the temple and the Pharisees were still together, Jesus asked them, "What do you think of the promised Savior? Whose Son is He?"

"David's," they answered Him.

"How can the Bible scholars say the promised Savior is David's Son?" He asked them. "David himself by the Holy Spirit calls Him Lord in the book of Psalms when he says,

The Lord said to my Lord,
'Sit at My right
Till I make Your enemies Your footstool.' [138]

Now, if David calls Him Lord, how can He be his Son?"

Nobody could answer Him.

Beware!

The big crowd liked to hear Him. As He taught and all the people were listening, Jesus said to the crowd and to His disciples, "Beware of the Bible scholars. They and the Pharisees sit in Moses' seat. Do everything they tell you, and follow it; but don't do what they do, because they don't do what they say. They tie together heavy loads that are hard to carry and lay them on the shoulders of others, but they won't raise a finger to move them.

"They do everything in order to be seen by others. They make their phylacteries broad and the tassels of their garments long.* They like the places of honor at dinners and the front seats in synagogs. They swallow the widows' houses and then, to cover up, make long prayers. They'll be punished all the more. They like to go around in long robes and to be greeted in the marketplaces and have people call them rabbi. But don't you let them call you rabbi, because you have only one Teacher, and you are all brothers. And don't call anyone on earth your father; you have only one Father, and He is in heaven. Don't have others call you teachers; you have only one Teacher, and that is Christ. The greatest among you will be one who serves you. If you honor yourself, you will be humbled, but if you humble yourself, you will be honored."

Woe!

"Woe to you Bible scholars and Pharisees, you hypocrites! You lock people out of the kingdom of heaven. You won't come into it yourselves, and when others try to come in, you won't let them.

"Woe to you Bible scholars and Pharisees, you hypocrites!

* A phylactery was a small leather box fastened by a leather strap on the forehead or on the left arm. In the box were pieces of parchment on which were written the words of Ex. 13:1-10, 11-16; Deut. 6:4-9, 13-21. — An Israelite wore a tassel on each of the four corners of his outer garment. (Num. 15:38-40; Deut. 22:12)

You go around lake and land to convert a single person, and when he's converted, you make him twice as fit for hell as you are.

"Woe to you blind guides! You say, 'If anyone swears by the temple, that's nothing. But if anyone swears by the gold in the temple, he must keep his oath.' Blind fools! Which is greater, the gold or the temple that made the gold holy? Or again, 'If anyone swears by the altar, that's nothing. But if anyone swears by the gift that's on it, he must keep his oath.' You blind men! Which is greater, the gift or the altar that makes the gift holy? If you swear by the altar, you swear by it and by everything on it. If you swear by the temple, you swear by it and by Him who lives there. And if you swear by heaven, you swear by God's throne and by Him who is sitting on it.

"Woe to you Bible scholars and Pharisees, you hypocrites! You give a tenth of mint and dill and cummin but have neglected the more important things of the Law: to be just, merciful, and trustworthy. You should have done the one without neglecting the other. Blind guides! You strain out the gnat but swallow the camel.

"Woe to you Bible scholars and Pharisees, you hypocrites! You clean the outside of a cup and of a dish, but inside they're full of greed and uncontrolled lust. You blind Pharisee! First clean the inside of the cup and of the dish in order to make also the outside of it clean. Woe to you Bible scholars and Pharisees, you hypocrites! You're like whitewashed graves that look beautiful on the outside but inside are full of dead men's bones and every kind of decay. So on the outside you look good to people, but inside you're full of hypocrisy and crime.

"Woe to you Bible scholars and Pharisees, you hypocrites! You build the tombs of the prophets and decorate the graves of the righteous and say, 'If we had lived at the time of our fathers, we wouldn't have helped them murder the prophets.' And so you testify against yourselves that you are the sons of those who murdered the prophets. Go on, finish what your fathers started!

"You snakes! Brood of vipers! How can you escape being condemned to hell? That's why I'm sending you men to speak God's Word, men who are wise and know the Bible. Some of them you will kill and crucify. Others you will whip in your synagogs and hunt from town to town, so that all the innocent blood poured on the ground will come on you, from the blood of righteous Abel to the blood of Zechariah, Barachiah's son, whom you murdered between the holy place and the altar. I tell you, all this will certainly come on the people of today.

"Jerusalem, Jerusalem, you murder the prophets and stone those sent to you! How often I wanted to bring your children together as a hen gathers her chicks under her wings, but you didn't want to! Now your *house will be left* to you *a deserted place*.[139] I tell you, you will not see Me again till you say, *'Blessed is He who is coming in the Lord's name.'* "[140]

A Cent

As Jesus sat facing the contribution boxes, He was watching how people put money into them. Many rich people put in much. He saw a poor widow come and drop in two small coins, worth about a cent.

He called His disciples. "I tell you," He said to them, "this poor widow certainly put in more than all the others who put in money. All the others took some of what they had left over and dropped it in among the gifts. But she put in what she needed for herself, all she had — all she had to live on."

Death and Glory

Among those who came up to worship at the festival were some Greeks. They went to Philip (who was from Bethsaida in Galilee) and told him, "Sir, we want to see Jesus." Philip went and told Andrew. Andrew and Philip went and told Jesus.

Jesus answered them, "The time has come for the Son of Man to be glorified. Surely, I tell you, if a kernel of wheat doesn't fall into the ground and die, it will be just one kernel. But if it dies, it produces much grain. Love your life and lose it, but hate your life in this world, and you will keep it for an everlasting life. If you serve Me, follow Me; and where I am, there My servant will be. If you serve Me, the Father will honor you.

"*I am deeply troubled* [141] now. But what should I say? Father, save Me from what is going to happen? No! I came to suffer this now. Father, glorify Your name."

Then a voice came from heaven: "I have glorified My name and will glorify it again."

The crowd, which stood there and heard it, said it had thundered. Others said, "An angel talked to Him." Jesus explained: "That voice did not come for My benefit but for yours.

"Now this world is being judged; now the ruler of this world will be thrown out. And once I have been lifted up from the earth, I will draw all people to Me." He said this to indicate how He was going to die.

The Light

Then the crowd answered Him, "We've heard from the Bible the promised Savior lives forever. How, then, can You say the Son of Man must be lifted up? Who is this Son of Man?"

"The Light will be with you just a little longer," Jesus answered them. "Walk while you have the Light, or darkness will overtake you. If you walk in the dark, you don't know where you're going. While you have the Light, believe in the Light in order to become enlightened people."

After Jesus had said this, He went away and hid from them. Although they had seen Him do so many miracles, they wouldn't believe in Him — what the prophet Isaiah said had to come true:

Lord, who has believed what we preach?
And to whom has the Lord's arm been uncovered? [142]

And so they couldn't believe, because Isaiah also said,

He blinded their eyes
And dulled their minds
So that their eyes don't see,
Their minds don't understand,
And they don't turn and let Me heal them.[143]

Isaiah said this because he saw His glory and spoke of Him. And yet even many of the rulers believed in Him but wouldn't say so publicly, because the Pharisees would have put them out of the synagog. Yes, they loved to be praised by men more than by God.

Then Jesus called out, "If you believe in Me, you don't believe only in Me but in Him who sent Me. And if you see Me, you see Him who sent Me. I have come as a light into the world so that anyone who believes in Me will not have to stay in the dark. If anyone hears what I say but doesn't keep it, I don't condemn him, because I didn't come to condemn the world but to save the world. If anyone rejects Me and doesn't take to heart what I say, he has one that is condemning him. The Word that I spoke will condemn him on the last day, because what I said didn't come from Me, but the Father who sent Me ordered Me to say and tell it. I know what He orders is everlasting life. And so, whatever I say, I say it just as the Father told Me."

The Temple Will Be Destroyed

When Jesus walked out of the temple and was going away, His disciples came to show Him the buildings of the temple. "Teacher," one of His disciples said to Him, "look at those wonderful stones and buildings!" And some were saying about the temple, "It is beautifully constructed with fine stones and gifts."

"You see all these large buildings?" Jesus asked them. "I tell you the truth: The time will come when not a stone will be left on another here but will be torn down."

Sorrow Ahead!

When He was sitting on the Mount of Olives, facing the temple, Peter, James, John, and Andrew came to Him alone. "Teacher," they asked Him, "tell us, when will this be, and how can we tell when all this is going to happen, when You're coming back and the world will come to an end?"

"Be careful not to let anyone deceive you," Jesus answered them. "Many will come using My name and saying, 'I am Christ,' and, 'The time has come,' and will deceive many. Don't follow them.

"You will hear of wars, rumors of wars, and revolutions. See that you don't get alarmed. These things *must happen* [144] first, but the end won't come right away."

Then He told them, "*Nation will fight against nation*, and *kingdom against kingdom*.[145] There will be great earthquakes and famines and plagues in different places, terrible sights and great signs coming from heaven. But all these are only the first pains. *

"Be on your guard! Before all these things happen, men will arrest you and persecute you, hand you over to their courts and church councils, and put you in prisons. They will whip you in their synagogs. They'll bring you before kings and governors on account of My name. It will be your chance to tell them the truth.

"This good news of the Kingdom must be preached all over the world so that all nations hear the truth, and then the end will come.

---

* As in childbirth, sharper pains will follow before the Savior comes in glory.

"When they are taking you away to hand you over to the authorities, make up your minds not to worry beforehand how you'll defend yourselves. But say whatever is given you to say when the time comes; I'll give you such speech and wisdom none of your enemies will be able to oppose it or talk against it. You see, it isn't you speaking but the Holy Spirit.

"They will kill you, and all nations will hate you on account of My name. Then *many will fall away* [146] and betray one another and hate one another. Even parents, brothers, relatives, and friends will betray you and kill some of you. A brother will betray his brother to death, and a father his child. *Children will rebel against their parents* [147] and kill them. Many false prophets will arise and lead many people astray. And because there will be more and more wickedness, the love of most people will turn cold.

"But not a hair on your head will be lost. Endure patiently to the end, and you'll win your lives and be saved."

Jerusalem Will Be Destroyed

"When you see Jerusalem surrounded by an army and what the prophet Daniel told about, *the abomination laying waste the land* and standing *in the holy place*,[148] where it should not be (anyone who reads this should understand it), then know the time has come for her to be destroyed. Then if you're in Judea, flee to the hills. If you're in Jerusalem, leave it. If you're in the country, don't go into the city. If you're on the roof, don't come down and go into your house to get anything. If you're in the field, don't turn back to get your garment. Those will be *days of vengeance* [149] when everything must happen as it is written.

"Woe to the women who in those days are expecting babies or nursing them. Pray that it may not be winter or a Sabbath when you flee. It will be a time of great *misery such as never has been from the beginning* of the world that God made *until now* [150] and never will be. And if the Lord had not cut short that time, nobody would be saved. But to help those whom He has chosen, God has cut short the time.

"There will be great distress in this country, and God will punish this nation. The sword will cut them down, they'll be taken away as prisoners among all nations, and *the Gentiles will trample on Jerusalem* [151] till the time for the Gentiles has passed."

Jesus Will Come Again

"The time will come," He told the disciples, "when you will long to see one of the days of the Son of Man and will not see it. If anyone tells you then, 'Look, here is Christ!' or, 'There He is!' don't believe it. Don't go off and run after them, because false Christs and false *prophets* will *come and do* great *miracles and wonders* [152] to deceive if possible even those whom God has chosen. Be on your guard. You see, I've told you everything before it happens. So when you're told, 'There He is in the wilderness,' don't go out; or, 'Here He is in the inner rooms,' don't believe it. The Son of Man will come like the lightning that flashes from the east to the west and lights up the sky from one end to the other. (Where the dead body is, there the vultures will gather.) But first He must suffer much and be rejected by these people.

"Right after the misery of that time there will be signs. *The sun will turn dark, the moon will stop shining, and the stars will be falling from the sky.* [153] And on the earth *nations* will be in distress, not knowing which way to turn from *the roaring and tossing of the sea.* [154] People will faint as they fearfully wait for what will happen to the world. *The powers of the heavens* [155] will be shaken. Then the sign announcing the Son of Man will appear in the sky, and then *all the people on earth will mourn* [156] when they see *the Son of Man coming on the clouds in the sky* [157] with great power and glory. And *with a loud trumpet call* [158] He will send out His angels, and they *will gather* His chosen ones *from the north, south, east, and west, from one end of the sky to the other.*[159]

"When these things begin to happen, stand ready and look forward cheerfully because you will soon be set free."

Then He pictured it this way: "Look at a fig tree, or any of the trees, and learn this lesson: When its branch gets tender and grows leaves, you see and know without being told that summer is near. So also when you see those things happen, you know God's kingdom is near and He is at your door.

"I tell you the truth: These people will not pass away till all this happens. Heaven and earth will pass away, but what I say will not pass away."

People Will Not Expect Him

"No one knows about that day or hour, not the angels in heaven, not even the Son, but only the Father.

"When the Son of Man comes, it will be like the time of Noah. In the days before the flood, they were eating and drinking, and men and women were marrying till the day *Noah went into the ark.* They learned nothing till *the flood came*[160] and swept them all away. That's how it will be when the Son of Man comes.

"Or like the time of Lot: They were eating and drinking, buying and selling, planting and building. But the day Lot left Sodom, *fire and sulfur rained from heaven and destroyed*[161] them all. That is how it will be on the day the Son of Man is revealed.

"On that day, if you're on the roof and have your goods in the house, don't go down to get them. If you're in the field, don't *turn back.* Remember *Lot's wife!*[162] If you try to save your life, you'll lose it, but if you'll lose it, you'll save it.

"I tell you, that night there will be two men in one bed — one will be taken and the other left. There will be two men in the field — one will be taken and the other left. Two women will be grinding together at a mill — one will be taken and the other left."

They asked Him, "Where, Lord?"

"Where there's a dead body," He told them, "there the vultures will gather."

Be Ready!

"Be careful and watch, because you don't know when it will happen. It's like a man who went on a trip. As he left home, he put his slaves in charge, assigned work to every one, and ordered the doorkeeper to watch. Watch, then, because you don't know when the master of the house is coming, whether in the evening, at midnight, at the time when the rooster crows, or early in the morning. Make sure he doesn't come suddenly and find you asleep. What I tell you, I tell everyone: 'Watch!' Be ready for action with belts fastened and lamps burning, like men waiting for their master when he comes back from a wedding, so they can open the door for him the moment he comes and knocks. Happy are those slaves whom the master finds watching when he comes. I tell you he'll certainly fasten his belt, have them lie down for a meal, and come and serve them. Even if he comes in the middle of the night or toward morning and finds them that way, happy are they.

"You know if the owner of a house had known what time of the night the burglar was coming, he would have stayed awake and not let anyone break into his house. You, too, get ready, because the Son of Man is coming when you don't expect Him."

"Lord," Peter asked, "by this illustration do you mean to warn us — or everybody else too?"

The Lord asked, "Who do you suppose is the manager that can be trusted and has good sense whom the master has put in charge of his servants to give them their share of food at the right time? Happy is that slave whom his master finds doing just this when he comes. I tell you he certainly will make him manager of all his property. But if that slave is wicked and says to himself, 'My master isn't coming back for some time,' and starts to beat the other slaves, men and women, and eats, drinks, and gets drunk with the drunkards, the master of that slave will come one day when he's not expecting him and at a time he doesn't know and will cut him in pieces and put him with the unfaithful, with the hypocrites. There they will cry and grind their teeth.

"That slave who knew what his master wanted and didn't prepare himself or do what he wanted will get many blows. But he who didn't know and did things for which he deserved to be beaten will get few blows. If you were given much, much will be expected of you, and if much was entrusted to you, all the more will be demanded of you.

"Be careful never to get your hearts burdened with drunkenness and its nausea and with worries about this life, or that day will take you by surprise like *a trap*. It will surprise all people wherever they *live on the earth*.[163] But always watch and pray to be considered worthy to escape all these things that are going to happen and to stand before the Son of Man."

The Bridegroom Is Coming

"Then the kingdom of heaven will be like ten girls who took their lamps and went out to meet the bridegroom. Five of them were foolish, and five were wise. The foolish girls brought their lamps, but they took no extra oil. The wise took flasks of oil with their lamps. But the bridegroom delayed, and so they all dozed off to sleep.

"At midnight there was a shout, 'Here's the bridegroom! Come out and meet him!' Then all those girls woke up and got their lamps ready.

"But the foolish asked the wise, 'Give us some of your oil. Our lamps are going out.'

"The wise girls answered, 'There will never be enough for us and for you. Better go to the dealers and buy some for yourselves.'

"While they were away buying it, the bridegroom came, and the girls who were ready went with him to the wedding, and the door was shut.

"Later the other girls also came and said, 'Lord, lord, open the door for us!'

"'I tell you the truth,' he answered them, 'I don't know you.'

"Keep awake, then, because you don't know the day or the hour."

Three Kinds of Workers

"It's like a man going on a trip. He called his slaves and put his money in their hands. He gave one man $10,000,* another $4,000, and another $2,000, each according to his ability. Then he left.

"The one who got $10,000 immediately went and put it into business and made another $10,000. The one who had $4,000 did the same and made another $4,000. But the one who got $2,000 went and dug a hole in the ground and hid his master's money.

"After a long time the master of those slaves came and had them give an account. The one who got $10,000 came and brought another $10,000. 'Master,' he said, 'you let me have $10,000. See, I've made another $10,000.'

"'Well done, good and faithful slave!' his master answered him. 'You proved you could be trusted with a little. I will put you in charge of something big. Come and be happy with your master.'

"The one who got $4,000 came and said, 'Master, you let me have $4,000. See, I've made another $4,000.'

---

* It is hard to estimate the real value of a "talent." It is here taken to be equal to $2,000.

"'Well done, good and faithful slave!' his master answered him. 'You proved you could be trusted with a little. I will put you in charge of something big. Come and be happy with your master.'

"Then came also the one who got $2,000. 'Master,' he said, 'I found out you're a hard man. You get grain where you didn't sow, and you gather where you didn't scatter. I was afraid, so I went and hid your $2,000 in the ground. There's your money!'

"'You wicked and lazy slave!' his master answered him. 'You knew I get grain where I didn't sow and gather where I didn't scatter? Then you should have invested my money with the bankers, and when I came back, I could have gotten my money back with interest. Take the $2,000 away from him, and give it to the one who has $10,000. Whoever has anything will receive, and so he will have more and more. And from him who doesn't have what he should have, even what he has will be taken away. Throw this good-for-nothing slave out into the dark where there will be crying and grinding of teeth.'"

Jesus Will Judge the World

"When the Son of Man *comes* in His glory *and all the* angels *with Him*,[164] then He will sit on His throne of glory. And all nations will be gathered before Him, and He will separate them from one another, as a shepherd separates the sheep from the goats, and He will have the sheep stand at His right but the goats at His left.

"Then the King will say to those at His right, 'Come, you whom My Father blessed, inherit the kingdom prepared for you from the time the world was made. I was hungry, and you gave Me something to eat; I was thirsty, and you gave Me a drink; I was a stranger, and you took Me into your homes; naked, and you gave Me something to wear; sick, and you looked after Me; in prison, and you visited Me.'

"Then the righteous will ask Him, 'Lord, when did we see

You hungry and feed You, or thirsty and give You a drink? When did we see You a stranger and take You into our homes, or naked and give You something to wear? When did we see You sick or in prison and visit You?'

"And the King will answer them, 'Let Me assure you, anything you did for one of My brothers here, however humble, you did for Me.'

"Then He will say to those at His left, 'Go away from Me, you cursed ones, into the everlasting fire prepared for the devil and his angels. I was hungry, and you gave Me nothing to eat; thirsty, and you didn't give Me a drink; a stranger, and you didn't take Me into your homes; naked, and you didn't give Me anything to wear; sick and in prison, and you didn't look after Me.'

"Then they too will ask, 'Lord, when did we see You hungry or thirsty or a stranger or naked or sick or in prison and didn't help You?'

"Then He will answer them, 'I tell you the truth, anything you didn't do for one of these, however humble, you didn't do for Me.'

"Then *these* will go away *to everlasting* punishment, but the righteous *to everlasting life.*" [165]

·10·
His Last Preparation

"I Will Betray Him"

The festival of bread without yeast, called the Passover, was near. Before the Passover festival Jesus knew the time had come for Him to leave this world and go to the Father. He had loved His own who were in the world, and now He loved them to the end. "You know that in two days the Passover will be celebrated," He said to His disciples, "and the Son of Man will be handed over to be crucified."

Then the ruling priests, the elders of the people, and the Bible scholars met in the palace of the high priest, whose name was Caiaphas. They were looking for some treacherous way to arrest Jesus and kill Him. They were afraid of the people. So they said, "Not in the festival crowd, or there may be a riot among the people."

The devil went into Judas, called the man from Kerioth, one of the twelve. He went to the high priests and the captains of the temple and discussed with them how he might betray Jesus to them. "What will you give me?" he asked. "I will betray Him to you."

They were delighted to hear it. They agreed to give him some money, and they *weighed out thirty shekels* * *of silver* [166] for him.

He promised to do it. And so from then on he was looking for a chance to betray Him when He was away from the crowd.

The Passover

Then came the first of the Passover days of bread without yeast, when the Passover lamb had to be killed, and the disciples came to Jesus. He sent two of His disciples, Peter and John, saying, "Go, get the Passover ready for us to eat."

The disciples asked Him, "Where do You want us to go and get things ready for You to eat the Passover?"

"Go into the city," He told them, "and you'll meet a man carrying a jar of water. Follow him into the house he enters, and tell the owner of the house: 'The Teacher says, "My time is near. I'm going to celebrate the Passover with My disciples at your house. Where is My room in which I can eat the Passover with My disciples?" ' Then he will show you a large room upstairs, furnished and ready. Get the things ready for us there."

The disciples did as Jesus directed them. They left, went into the city, and found everything as He had told them. And so they got the Passover ready.

In the evening, when the hour had come, He came there with the twelve apostles and lay down for the supper. "I have very much longed to eat this Passover with you before I suffer," He said to them. "I tell you, I will not eat it again till it comes true in God's kingdom.' Then He was handed a cup, and He gave thanks. "Take this," He said, "and share it."

---

* A silver shekel weighed as much as our half dollar.

Jesus Washes the Disciples' Feet

It was during the supper. The devil had already put the idea of betraying Jesus into the mind of Judas, the son of Simon from Kerioth.

Jesus knew the Father put everything into His hands and He had come from God and was going back to God.

Then the disciples started to quarrel among themselves as to which of them was considered the greatest.

So Jesus rose from supper, laid aside His outer garment, took a towel, and tied it around Him. Then He poured water into a basin and started to wash the disciples' feet and to dry them with the towel that was tied around Him.

And so He came to Simon Peter. "Lord," Peter asked Him, "are You going to wash my feet?"

"You don't know now what I'm doing," Jesus answered him. "But later you will understand."

"No!" Peter told Him. "You'll never wash my feet."

"If I don't wash you," Jesus answered him, "you have no share in Me."

"Lord," Simon Peter told Him, "not only my feet but also my hands and my head."

"Anyone who has bathed needs only to have his feet washed," Jesus told him. "He's clean all over. You're clean, but not all of you." He knew who was betraying Him. That's why He said, "Not all of you are clean."

After He had washed their feet and put on His garment, He lay down again. "Do you know what I've done to you?" He asked them. "You call Me Teacher and Lord, and you're right, because I am that. Now if I, the Lord and the Teacher, have washed your feet, you too should wash one another's feet. I've given you an example so that you will do as I did to you. Surely, I tell you, a slave is no greater than his master, and if you're sent, you're no greater than he who sent you. If you know this, you're happy if you do it.

"The kings of the nations lord it over them, and their rulers call themselves benefactors. With you it's different. The greatest among you should become like the youngest, and one who leads should be like one who serves. Who is greater, the one who lies down to eat or the one who serves? Isn't it the one who lies down to eat? But I am among you as one who serves.

"You have stood by Me in the troubles that have tested Me. As My Father has appointed Me to be King, so I appoint you to eat and drink at My table in My kingdom and to sit on thrones and rule the twelve tribes of Israel.

"I'm not talking about all of you. I know whom I've chosen. But what the Bible says has to come true: *He who eats My bread kicks Me.*[167] From now on I'm telling you these things before they happen so that when they happen you believe I am the One.

"Let Me assure you, if you receive anyone I send, you receive Me, and if you receive Me, you receive Him who sent Me."

"Is It I?"

After saying this, and while they were still lying down and eating, Jesus was deeply troubled. "I tell you the truth," He declared, "one of you is going to betray Me, one who is *eating with Me!* [167] Look, the hand of him who is betraying Me is with Me on the table."

The disciples started to look at one another, wondering whom He meant, and to discuss with one another which of them was going to do this. Feeling deeply hurt, they asked Him one after another, "You don't mean me, Lord?"

"One of the twelve," He answered them, "one who is dipping into the bowl with Me will betray Me. The Son of Man is going away as it is decreed and written about Him, but woe to that man who betrays the Son of Man! It would be better for that man if he had never been born."

One of His disciples, the one Jesus loved, was lying close to Jesus' bosom. Simon Peter motioned to him to ask whom He meant.

Leaning back, where he was, against Jesus' breast, he asked Him, "Lord, who is it?"

"I'll dip this piece of bread and give it to him," Jesus answered. "He's the one." Then he dipped it and gave it to Judas, the son of Simon from Kerioth.

"You don't mean me, Master?" asked Judas, who was going to betray Him.

"I do!" He told him.

After Judas took the piece of bread, the devil went into him. So Jesus told him, "What you're doing, do quickly." What He meant by telling him this, nobody at the table knew. Some thought, since Judas had the money box, Jesus was telling him, "Buy what we need for the festival," or that he should give something to the poor.

Right after taking the piece of bread Judas went outside. And it was night.

When Judas had gone out, Jesus said, "Now the Son of Man is glorified, and in Him God is glorified. God will also glorify Him in Himself; yes, He will glorify Him now."

The Lord's Supper

In the night in which He was betrayed, while they were eating, the Lord Jesus took bread and gave thanks. He broke it and gave it to the disciples and said, "Take and eat. This is My body, which is given for you. Do this to remember Me."

In the same way He took a cup when the supper was over and gave thanks. He gave it to them, saying, "Drink of it, all of you." And they all drank of it. He told them, "This is My *blood of the new covenant,*[168] poured out for you and for all to forgive their sins. Do this, as often as you drink it, to remember Me.

"Surely, I tell you, I will not drink again of this product

of the vine till that day when I drink it with you in a new way in the kingdom of God, My Father."

Then they sang a hymn. *

Jesus Warns Peter

"Children," Jesus said, "I'm with you just a little longer. You will look for Me, but as I told the Jews, so I tell you now: Where I'm going, you can't come.

"I'm giving you a new order: Love one another! Love one another as I have loved you. By your loving one another everybody will know you're My disciples."

"Lord, where are You going?" Simon Peter asked Him.

"Where I'm going, you can't follow Me now," Jesus answered him; "but you will follow Me later."

"Lord, why can't I follow You now?" Peter asked Him.

"Simon, Simon," said the Lord, "you know the devil has begged to have all of you to sift you like wheat. But I prayed for you, Simon, that your faith will not die. And when you come back, strengthen your fellow disciples."

"Lord," he told Him, "I'm ready to go to prison and to die with You. I'll give my life for You."

"You'll give your life for Me?" Jesus asked. "I tell you the truth, Peter, the rooster will not crow tonight till you deny three times that you know Me."

Then He asked them, "When I sent you out without purse, bag, or shoes, you didn't lack anything, did you?"

"Not a thing!" they answered.

"But now," He told them, "if you have a purse, take it, and also a bag. And if you don't have a sword, sell your garment and buy one. It is written, *He will be counted among criminals*,[169] and I tell you, that must happen to Me. Whatever is written about Me must happen!"

"Lord, look, here are two swords!" they said.

"Enough of that!" He told them.

* Perhaps Psalms 115—118.

"I Am the Way"

"Don't feel troubled. Believe in God, and believe in Me. In My Father's house there are many rooms. If it were not so, I would have told you, because I go to prepare a place for you. And when I have gone and prepared a place for you, I'll come again and take you home with Me so you'll be where I am. You know the way to the place where I'm going."

"Lord, we don't know where You're going," Thomas said to Him. "So how can we know the way?"

"I am the Way, the Truth, and the Life," Jesus answered him. "No one comes to the Father except by Me. If you have learned to know Me, you'll know My Father too. From now on you know Him and have seen Him."

Philip said to Him, "Lord, show us the Father; that's enough for us."

"I've been with all of you so long," Jesus answered him, "and you don't know Me, Philip? If you have seen Me, you have seen the Father. How can you say, 'Show us the Father'? Don't you believe I am in the Father and the Father is in Me? What I tell you doesn't come from Me, but the Father, who lives in Me, is doing His works. Believe Me, I am in the Father, and the Father is in Me. Or else believe Me on account of My works.

"I tell you the truth, if you believe in Me, you'll do the works I'm doing, and you'll do greater works than these, because I'm going to the Father, and I will do anything you ask in My name in order that the Son may glorify the Father. If you ask Me for anything in My name, I'll do it.

"If you love Me, you will do what I order. And I will ask the Father, and He will give you another Comforter to be with you forever. He is the Spirit of truth, whom the world cannot receive, because it doesn't see or know Him. You know Him, because He lives with you and will be in you.

"I will not leave you orphans; I'm coming back to you. Only a little while and the world won't see Me anymore. But you will see Me, because I live, and you too will live. On that day you will know I'm in My Father and you in Me and I in you. If you have My commandments and obey them, you love Me. And if you love Me, My Father will love you, and I will love you and show Myself to you."

Judas (not the man from Kerioth) asked Him, "Lord, what has happened that You're going to show Yourself to us and not to the world?"

Jesus answered him, "If you love Me, you'll do what I say, and My Father will love you, and We will come to you and live with you. Anyone who doesn't love Me doesn't do what I say. And you are hearing, not what I say but what the Father says who sent Me.

"I've told you this while I'm still with you. But the Comforter, the Holy Spirit, whom the Father will send in My name, will teach you everything and remind you of everything I told you.

"I leave peace with you, I give you My peace. I don't give it to you as the world gives it. Don't feel troubled or afraid. You heard Me tell you, 'I'm going away, but I'm coming back to you.' If you loved Me, you'd be glad I'm going to the Father, because the Father is greater than I.

"I've told you this now before it happens, so that when it happens, you believe. I won't say much to you anymore, because the ruler of the world is coming. He has no claim on Me. But I want the world to know I love the Father and am doing just what the Father ordered Me to do.

"Come, let us go away."

Vine and Branch

"I am the real Vine, and My Father takes care of the vineyard. He cuts away any branch of Mine that bears no fruit, and He trims any branch that bears fruit to make it bear more fruit.

"What I have said to you has already made you clean.

Stay in Me, and I will stay in you. A branch can't bear any fruit by itself — if it doesn't stay in the vine. Neither can you if you don't stay in Me. I am the Vine, you are the branches. If you stay in Me and I in you, you bear much fruit. Without Me you can't do anything. If anyone doesn't stay in Me, he's thrown away like a branch and dries up. Such branches are gathered, thrown into the fire, and burned. If you stay in Me and what I say stays in you, ask for anything you want, and it will be done for you. You glorify My Father when you bear much fruit and so prove to be My disciples. As the Father has loved Me, so I have loved you. Stay in My love. If you obey My commandments, you'll stay in My love, as I have obeyed My Father's commandments and stay in His love. I told you this so that My joy will be in you and you will be very happy. This is what I order you to do: Love one another as I have loved you. No one has a greater love than he who gives his life for his friends. You're My friends if you do what I order you to do. I don't call you servants anymore, because a servant doesn't know what his master is doing. But I've called you friends, because I've told you everything I heard from My Father. You didn't choose Me, but I chose you and appointed you to go and bear fruit that doesn't pass away and to have the Father give you anything you ask Him in My name. This is what I order you to do: Love one another.

"If the world hates you, you know it hated Me first. If you belonged to the world, the world would love you as its own. But you don't belong to the world; I took you away from the world; that's why the world hates you. Remember what I told you: a slave is no greater than his Master. If they persecuted Me, they'll persecute you. If they did what I said, they'll do what you say. Now they will do all this to you on account of Me, because they don't know Him who sent Me. If I hadn't come and spoken to them, they wouldn't be sinning, but now they have no excuse for their sin. Anyone who hates Me hates My Father. If I hadn't done among them the works no one else has done, they wouldn't be sinning. But now they have seen and hated Me and My Father. What is written in their Bible has to come true: *They will hate Me without any reason.*[170]

"When the Comforter comes, whom I'll send you from the Father, the Spirit of truth, who comes from the Father, He'll tell the truth about Me. And you too tell the truth, because you've been with Me from the beginning."

Sorrow Will Turn to Joy

"I told you this so that nothing will upset your faith. You will be put out of the synagog. Yes, the time will come when anyone who murders you will think he's serving God. Men will do these things because they didn't get to know the Father or Me. But I told you this so that when it happens you'll remember I told you about it. I didn't tell you this at first, because I was with you.

"Now I'm going to Him who sent Me, and none of you asks Me, 'Where are You going?' But because I told you this, you feel very sad. But I tell you the truth, it's good for you that I go away. If I don't go away, the Comforter will not come to you. But if I go, I'll send Him to you. He will come and convict the world of sin, righteousness, and judgment: of sin because they don't believe in Me; of righteousness because I'm going to the Father and you won't see Me anymore; of judgment because the ruler of this world is judged.

"I have much more to tell you, but it would be too much for you now. When the Spirit of truth comes, He will lead you into the whole truth. What He will say will not come from Himself, but He'll speak what He hears and tell you what is coming. He will glorify Me, because He'll take from what is Mine and tell it to you. Everything the Father has is Mine. That is why I said, 'He takes from what is Mine and will tell it to you.'

"A little while and you'll not see Me anymore; and again a little while and you'll see Me."

Then some of His disciples asked one another, "What does He mean when He tells us, 'Just a little while and you'll not see Me; and again only a little while and you'll see Me,' and, 'I'm going to the Father'?" So they were asking, "What does He mean when He says, 'A little while'? We don't know what He means."

Jesus knew they wanted to ask Him something. "Are you trying to find out from one another," He asked them, "what I meant by saying, 'A little while and you'll not see Me; and again a little while and you'll see Me'? I tell you the truth, you will cry and mourn, but the world will be glad. You will have sorrow, but your sorrow will turn to joy. When a woman is going to have a child, she has pains because her time has come. But after the child is born, she's so happy a child was brought into the world she doesn't remember her pains anymore. You too are sad now; but I'll see you again, *and then you'll be glad*,[171] and nobody will take your joy away from you. Then you won't ask Me any questions. I tell you the truth, if you ask the Father for anything, He will give it to you in My name. So far you haven't asked for anything in My name. Ask and you will receive and be very happy.

"I used veiled speech in telling you these things. The time is coming when I won't use veiled speech anymore in talking to you, but I'll tell you about the Father in plain words. Then you will ask in My name, and I don't tell you I'll ask the Father for you. The Father Himself loves you because you have loved Me and believe that I came from the Father. I left the Father and came into the world; and now I'm leaving the world again and going to the Father."

"Yes, now You're talking in plain words," His disciples said, "and using no veiled speech. Now we know You know everything and don't need to have anyone ask You anything. That's why we believe You've come from God."

"Now you believe," Jesus answered them. "The hour is coming, in fact, it's here now, when you'll be scattered, everyone to his home, and you'll leave Me alone. But I'm not alone, because the Father is with Me. I told you this so you will have peace in Me. In the world you have trouble. But have courage; I've conquered the world."

Jesus Prays

After saying this, Jesus looked up to heaven and said:

"Father, the time has come. Glorify Your Son so that Your Son will glorify You, since You have given Him power over all men, to give everlasting life to all whom You gave Him. This is everlasting life — to know You, the only true God, and Jesus Christ, whom You sent. I have glorified You on earth by finishing the work You gave Me to do. And now, Father, glorify Me at Your side with the glory I had with You before the world began.

"I made Your name known to the people You gave Me out of the world. They were Yours, and You gave them to Me, and they have kept Your Word. Now they know everything You gave Me comes from You, because I gave them the message You gave Me. And they have accepted it and learned the truth that I came from You, and have believed You sent Me.

"I pray for them. I don't pray for the world but for those You gave Me, because they are Yours. All that is Mine is Yours, and what is Yours is Mine. And I am glorified in them. I am no longer in the world, but they are in the world, and I am coming to You. Holy Father, keep them in Your name, which You gave Me, so that they will be one as We are one. While I was with them, I kept them safe in Your name, which You gave Me. I watched over them, and none of them was lost except that lost one — what the Bible says had to come true.

"But now I am coming to You, and I say this while I am in the world so that they will feel all My joy in their hearts.

I gave them Your Word. But the world has hated them because they don't belong to the world any more than I belong to the world. I'm not asking You to take them out of the world but to keep them from the evil one. They don't belong to the world any more than I belong to the world.

"Make them holy by the truth; Your Word is truth. As You sent Me into the world, I sent them into the world. In this holy way I give Myself for them to make them holy too by the truth. I'm not asking for them only but also for those who through their word believe in Me that they all be one. As You, Father, are in Me and I in You, let them be in Us so that the world may believe You sent Me. I gave them the glory You gave Me to make them one as We are one. I am in them, and You are in Me to make them perfectly one that the world may know You sent Me and loved them as You loved Me.

"Father, I want those You gave Me to be with Me where I am and to see My glory that You gave Me because You loved Me before the world was made. Righteous Father, the world didn't know You, but I knew You, and these have learned to know You sent Me. I told them and I am going to tell them Your name, so that the love You have for Me will be in them and I will be in them."

· 11 ·

Our Suffering Savior

"You Will Deny Me"

After Jesus said this, they started out for the Mount of Olives.

Then Jesus told them, "Tonight you will all turn against Me. It is written: I will *strike down the Shepherd, and the sheep of the flock will be scattered.*[172] But after I have risen, I will go ahead of you to Galilee."

"Even if they all turn against You," Peter answered Him, "I'll never turn against You."

"I tell you the truth," Jesus told him, "tonight, before the rooster crows twice, you will deny Me three times."

But Peter kept insisting all the more, "Even if I have to die with You, I'll never deny You!" All the other disciples said the same thing.

Gethsemane

Jesus took His disciples as usual to the other side of the Kidron valley and went with them to a place called Gethsemane.

"Sit down here while I go over there and pray," He told them. "Pray that you may not be tempted." He withdrew from them about as far as you'd throw a stone.

Taking Peter and Zebedee's two sons, James and John, with Him, He started to feel terror and grief. Then He said to them, "*I am* so *full of sorrow* [173] I am almost dying. Stay here and keep awake with Me."

Going ahead a little, He bowed down with His face to the ground and prayed that if it were possible He might not have to suffer what was ahead of Him. "My Father," He said, "You can do anything. If it is possible and if You wish, take this cup away from Me; but let it not be as I want it but as You want it."

An angel from heaven appeared to Him and gave Him strength. And as He began to struggle inwardly, He prayed more earnestly, and His sweat became like thick drops of blood falling on the ground. *

After praying, He got up, went to the disciples, and found them sleeping because they were feeling sad. "Simon, are you sleeping?" He asked Peter. Then He said to them, "So you couldn't keep awake with Me one hour! Why are you sleeping? Get up, stay awake, and pray that you may not be tempted. The spirit is willing, but the flesh is weak."

Then He went away a second time and prayed the same as before: "My Father, if this cannot pass by without My drinking it, Your will be done."

He came again and found them asleep — they couldn't keep their eyes open and didn't know what to say to Him.

Leaving them again, He went and prayed the same

* Papyrus 75 and some other old manuscripts omit this paragraph.

prayer a third time. Then He came to the disciples the third time. "Are you going to sleep on now and rest?" He asked them. "It's enough. The time has come. Now the Son of Man will be betrayed into the hands of sinners. Get up, let us go. Here comes the man to betray Me!"

Judas Betrays Jesus

Judas, one of the twelve, who was betraying Him, also knew the place because Jesus and His disciples often got together there. So Judas took the troop of soldiers and servants from the ruling priests, the Bible scholars, and the elders of the people. Just then, while Jesus was still talking, they came there, a large crowd, with lanterns and torches, swords and clubs. The traitor had given them a signal. "The One I kiss is the Man," he said. "Grab Him, take Him away, and don't let Him escape."

Then Jesus went out, knowing exactly what was going to happen to Him. "Whom are you looking for?" He asked them.

"Jesus from Nazareth," they answered Him.

"I am He," Jesus told them.

Judas, ready to betray Him, was standing with them. When Jesus told them, "I am He," they went backward and fell to the ground.

He asked them again, "Whom are you looking for?"

"Jesus from Nazareth," they said.

"I told you I am He," Jesus answered. "So if I'm the One you want, let these others go." This was to make good what He had said: "I lost none of those You gave Me." *

Then Judas, who was leading them, quickly stepped up to Jesus and said, "Greetings, Master!" and kissed Him.

"Friend, what are you here for?" Jesus asked him. "Judas, are you betraying the Son of Man with a kiss?"

* See John 6:39; 17:12.

The Arrest

The men around Jesus, seeing what was going to happen, asked, "Lord, should we strike with our swords?"

Then the others came forward, took hold of Jesus, and arrested Him.

Simon Peter, who was standing near Jesus, reached for his sword and drew it. He struck the high priest's slave and cut off his right ear. The slave's name was Malchus.

But Jesus said, "Let them do it. No more of this!" And, touching the ear, He healed him.

"Put your sword back into its scabbard," Jesus told Peter. "All who take the sword must die by the sword. Or do you think I couldn't call on My Father to send right now more than seventy thousand angels to help Me? How, then, could the Bible be true when it says this must happen? The cup My Father gave Me — shouldn't I drink it?"

Then Jesus said to the crowd of ruling priests, captains of the temple, and elders who had come for Him, "Did you come out to arrest Me with swords and clubs as if I were a robber? Day after day I was with you as I sat and taught in the temple, and you laid no hands on Me and didn't arrest Me. But this is your time when darkness rules. All this has happened so that what the prophets have written would come true."

Then all the disciples left Him and ran away. One young man who also was following Him had nothing on but a linen cloth. They tried to grab him, but he left the linen cloth and ran away naked.

So the troop of soldiers, the tribune, and the attendants of the Jews arrested Jesus, bound Him, led Him away, and took Him to the high priest's palace. They took Him first to Annas, because he was the father-in-law of Caiaphas, who was high priest that year. It was Caiaphas who advised the Jews, "It is better that one man dies instead of the people."

Peter Follows Jesus

Now, Simon Peter and another disciple were following Jesus at a distance. The other disciple was known to the high priest and went with Jesus into the high priest's courtyard. But Peter was standing outside the door. So the other disciple, whom the high priest knew, went out and talked to the girl watching the door and brought Peter into the high priest's courtyard.

The slaves and the attendants were standing around and had lit a fire in the middle of the courtyard and made a heap of burning coals because it was cold. As they sat together and warmed themselves, Peter was standing and sitting with the attendants and warming himself at the fire. He wanted to see how this would end.

Before Annas

Then the high priest asked Jesus about His disciples and His teaching.

"I have spoken publicly to the world," Jesus answered him. "I have always taught in a synagog or in the temple, where all the Jews gather, and I haven't said anything in secret. Why do you ask Me? Ask those who heard Me what I said to them; they know what I said."

When He said this, one of the attendants standing near Jesus slapped His face. "Is that how You answer the high priest?" he asked.

"If I said anything wrong," Jesus answered him, "tell us what was wrong. But if I told the truth, why do you hit Me?"

Then Annas sent Him, still bound, to Caiaphas, the high priest.

First Trial Before the Jewish Court

All the ruling priests, elders, and Bible scholars had been called together.

The ruling priests and the whole Jewish court tried to get false testimony against Jesus in order to kill Him but couldn't find any. Although many came forward and gave false testimony against Him, their statements didn't agree.

At last two men came forward and gave this false testimony against Him: "We heard Him say, 'I can tear down God's temple and build it in three days'; 'I will tear down this temple, made by human hands, and in three days build another not made by human hands.'" But even on this point their statements didn't agree.

Then the high priest stepped forward. "Don't You have anything to say to this?" he asked Jesus. "What are these men testifying against You?"

But Jesus was silent and didn't answer.

Again the high priest asked Him, "Swear by the living God, and tell us, are You the promised Savior, the Son of God, the Son of the Blessed?"

"I am," Jesus said. "But I tell you, from now on you will all see *the Son of Man sitting at the right hand* of power and *coming in the clouds of heaven.*" [174]

Then the high priest tore his robes. "He has blasphemed!" he declared. "Why do we need any more witnesses? You just heard the blasphemy. What's your verdict?"

Then all condemned Him. "He must die!" they answered.

Then some of them started to spit in His face. The men who were holding Him were making fun of Him. They covered His face, struck Him with their fists, and some slapped Him, saying, "Prophesy, You Christ, and tell us: Who hit You?" And so they went on insulting Him in many other ways. The attendants also slapped Him when they took charge of Him.

Peter Denies Jesus

Peter was sitting outside, down in the courtyard. As he sat in the light of the fire, the doorkeeper, one of the high priest's maids, came and saw Peter warming himself. She came to him and asked, "You aren't one of this Man's disciples too, are you?"

"I'm not," he answered.

"You too were with the Man from Nazareth — this Jesus, the Galilean," she said, looking straight at him. "He too was with Him."

But he denied it in front of all of them: "I don't know Him, woman, and I don't know what you're talking about."

A little later he went out to the entrance. Then a rooster crowed.

Another maid saw him. "He was with Jesus from Nazareth," she also told those who were standing around.

Simon Peter continued to stand and warm himself. So the men asked him, "You aren't one of His disciples too, are you?" A little later someone else looked at him and said, "You're one of them."

Again Peter denied, and he swore, "Man, I'm not! I don't know the Man!"

About an hour later another insisted: "Certainly he was with Him. Why, he's a Galilean!" Those who stood near him came and also told Peter, "Sure, you're one of them. Anyone can tell by the way you talk. You're a Galilean!" One of the high priest's slaves, a relative of the man whose ear Peter had cut off, asked, "Didn't I see you with Him in the garden?"

Again Peter denied, "Man, I don't know what you're talking about." Then he started to curse and swear, "I don't know this Man you're talking about." Just then, while he was still speaking, a rooster crowed a second time.

Then the Lord turned and looked at Peter, and Peter remembered the Lord telling him, "Before the rooster crows twice today, you will deny Me three times." And he went outside and started to cry bitterly.

Second Meeting of the Jewish Court

As soon as it was morning, all the ruling priests and the elders of the people and the Bible scholars, that is, the whole Jewish court, had a meeting. They brought Jesus before their court and asked, "Are You the promised Savior? Tell us."

"If I tell you, you won't believe Me," He said to them. "And if I ask you a question, you won't answer. But from now on *the Son of Man* will be *sitting at the right of God's*[174] power."

"Are You, then, the Son of God?" all of them asked.

He answered them, "As you say: I am He."

"Why do we need any more testimony?" they asked. "We've heard Him say it ourselves."

Then the whole crowd of them decided to kill Jesus. They got up, bound Jesus, took Him from Caiaphas to the governor's palace, and handed Him over to Pilate, the governor. It was early in the morning.

Judas Hangs Himself

When Judas, who betrayed Him, saw that Jesus was condemned, he felt sorry and brought the thirty shekels of silver back to the high priests and elders. "I have sinned," he said. "I have betrayed innocent blood."

"What do we care about that?" they asked. "See to it yourself."

Then he threw the money into the temple and left. He went away and hanged himself. Falling on his face, he burst in the middle, and all his intestines poured out.

The high priests took the money. "It isn't right to put this into the temple treasury," they said; "it's blood money." So they decided to buy with it the potter's field for the burial of strangers. That's why that field has ever since been called the Field of Blood. Then what the prophet Jeremiah said came true: *I took the thirty shekels of silver, the price of Him on whom some* men of Israel *set a price, and I gave them for the potter's* field, *as the Lord directed me.*[175]

Before Pilate

To keep from getting unclean (they wanted to celebrate the Passover), the Jews themselves didn't go into the governor's palace. So Pilate came out to them. "What accusation are you bringing against this Man?" he asked.

"If He weren't a criminal," they answered him, "we wouldn't have handed Him over to you."

"Take Him yourselves," Pilate therefore told them, "and judge Him according to your law."

"We're not allowed to kill anyone," the Jews answered him. And so what Jesus said when He predicted how He would die was to come true.

Then they started to accuse Him: "We found that He makes our people disloyal, keeps them from paying taxes to the emperor, and says He is Christ, a king."

Pilate went back into the palace and called for Jesus. Jesus stood before the governor. Pilate asked Him, "Are You the King of the Jews?"

"Did you think of that yourself," Jesus asked, "or did others tell you about Me?"

"Am I a Jew?" Pilate asked. "Your own people and the ruling priests handed You over to me. What did You do?"

"My kingdom is not of this world," Jesus answered. "If My kingdom were of this world, My servants would fight to keep Me from being handed over to the Jews. But now My kingdom is not of this world."

"Then You are a king?" Pilate asked Him.

"Yes, I am a king!" Jesus answered. "I was born and came into the world to testify to the truth. Everyone who lives in the truth listens to Me."

Pilate said to Him, "What is truth?" After saying this, he went out to the Jews again and told the ruling priests and the crowd, "I don't find this Man guilty of anything."

While the ruling priests and elders were accusing Him of many things, He said nothing.

"Don't You have anything to say to this?" Pilate asked Him again. "Don't you hear how many accusations they're bringing against You?"

But Jesus didn't answer him anymore in regard to anything that was said, so that Pilate was very much surprised.

Before Herod

The priests and the crowd kept urging him: "He stirs up the people by teaching all over the country of the Jews, beginning in Galilee and coming here."

When Pilate heard that, he asked, "Is the Man from Galilee?" And when he found out Jesus came from the country governed by Herod, he sent Him to Herod, who also was in Jerusalem at that time.

Herod was very glad to see Jesus. For a long time he wanted to see Him because he was hearing about Him, and he was expecting to see Jesus do some miracle. He asked Him a lot of questions, but Jesus didn't answer him. The ruling priests and the Bible scholars were standing there and accusing Him vehemently.

So Herod and his soldiers treated Him with contempt and made fun of Him. They put a splendid garment on Him and then sent Him back to Pilate. On that day Herod and Pilate became friends. Before this they had been enemies.

Then Pilate called the ruling priests, the other leaders, and the people together. "You brought me this Man as one who turns the people against the government," he told them. "And now look, I've examined this Man before you and found Him innocent of the things you accuse Him of. And Herod did too, because he sent Him back to us. You see, He hasn't done anything to deserve death. So I'm going to teach Him a lesson and let Him go."

Barabbas

Now, at every festival the governor used to free one prisoner whom the crowd wanted and asked for. Just then there was a well-known prisoner, a robber by the name of Barabbas. He had been put in prison with the rebels who had committed a murder in a revolt that had taken place in the city. And the crowd came up and asked Pilate to do for them as he had done before.

"You have a custom that I set someone free for you at the Passover," Pilate answered them. "Whom do you want me to set free for you, Barbabbas or Jesus, the King of the Jews, who is called Christ?" He knew the ruling priests had handed Jesus over to him because they were jealous.

While he was sitting on the judge's seat, his wife sent someone to tell him, "Let that righteous Man alone. I suffered much in a dream last night on account of Him."

But the ruling priests and elders stirred up the people to ask him to free Barabbas for them and kill Jesus.

"Which of the two," the governor asked them, "do you want me to set free for you?"

Then the whole crowd yelled: "Not this One! Away with Him! Free Barabbas for us!"

But Pilate wanted to let Jesus go, so he called to them again and asked them, "Then what should I do with Jesus, who is called Christ, whom you call the King of the Jews?"

Then all of them kept yelling: "Crucify, crucify Him!"

And Pilate spoke to them a third time: "Why, what wrong has He done? I haven't found anything in Him that deserves death. So I will teach Him a lesson and let Him go."

But they kept yelling all the louder, "Crucify Him! He must be crucified!" and their shouts were overpowering Pilate.

When he saw he wasn't getting anywhere, but a riot was breaking out instead, Pilate took water and washed his hands before the crowd. "I am innocent of this One's blood," he said. "See to it yourselves!"

And all the people answered, "His blood be on us and on our children."

Then Pilate, wanting to satisfy the people, decided what they demanded should be done: he let them have Barabbas, who had been put in prison for revolt and murder but whom they were asking for.

"Look at the Man!"

Then Pilate took Jesus and had Him scourged. Then the governor's soldiers took Jesus into the courtyard of the governor's palace and called together and gathered the whole troop of soldiers around Him.

The soldiers took off His clothes and put a scarlet cloak on Him. They twisted some thorns into a crown, placed it on His head, and put a stick in His right hand. Then they went up to Jesus, knelt before Him, and worshiped Him. In mockery they started to greet Him: "Hail, King of the Jews!" They spit on Him, took the stick and hit Him on the head with it, and slapped His face.

After they mocked Him, Pilate went outside again. "I'm bringing Him out to you," he told them, "to let you know I don't find Him guilty of anything." Jesus came outside wearing the crown of thorns and the purple cloak. "Look at the Man!" Pilate said to them.

When the ruling priests and the servants saw Him, they shouted, "Crucify, crucify Him!"

"Take Him yourselves," Pilate told them, "and crucify Him. I don't find Him guilty of anything."

"We have a law," the Jews answered him, "and according to the law He must die. He has claimed to be God's Son."

When Pilate heard them say that, he was frightened more than ever. He went into the palace again. "Where are You from?" he asked Jesus. But Jesus didn't answer him.

"Don't You speak to me?" Pilate then asked Him. "Don't You know I have the power to free You or to crucify You?"

"You wouldn't have any power over Me," Jesus answered him, "if it hadn't been given to you from above. That is why the man who handed Me over to you is guilty of a greater sin."

This made Pilate anxious to let Him go, but the Jews shouted, "If you let Him go, you're no friend of Caesar. Anyone who makes himself a king is against Caesar."

When Pilate heard this, he took Jesus outside and sat in the judge's seat at a place called Stone Pavement, or Gabbatha in the Jewish language. It was the Friday of the Passover and about six o'clock.

"Look at your King!" he said to the Jews.

Then they shouted, "Away with Him! Kill Him! Crucify Him!"

"Should I crucify your King?" Pilate asked them.

"We don't have any king but Caesar," the ruling priests answered.

Then Pilate handed Jesus over to them to be crucified — it was what they wanted.

On the Way

The soldiers took off the purple cloak and put His own clothes on Him. So they took Jesus and led Him out to crucify Him. He was carrying His cross.

Going out, they found a certain Simon from Cyrene, the father of Alexander and Rufus, on his way in from the country. And as he was going to pass by, they took hold of him, laid the cross on him, and forced him to carry it behind Jesus.

A large crowd of the people followed Him. The women in the crowd were beating their breasts and weeping over Him.

Turning to them, Jesus said, "Daughters of Jerusalem, don't cry over Me, but cry over yourselves and your children, because the time is coming when people will say:

'Happy are —
> the women who couldn't have children,
> the wombs that didn't bear,
> and the breasts that didn't nurse.'

Then people will say —
> *to the mountains: 'Fall on us!'*
> *and to the hills: 'Cover us!'* [176]

If this is done to the green tree, what will be done to a dry one?"

Two others, who were criminals, were also taken away to be killed with Him.

"They Crucified Him"

They took Him to what was called Skull Place, which the Jews call Golgotha.

They tried to give Him a drink of wine mixed with myrrh and *gall*,[177] but when He tasted it, He refused to drink it. They crucified Him there. Then they crucified two robbers with Him, one at His right and the other at His left and Jesus in the middle. It was nine in the morning when they crucified Him.

Then Jesus said, "Father, forgive them; they don't know what they are doing." *

When the soldiers had crucified Jesus, they took His clothes and divided them into four parts, one for each soldier, throwing lots for them to see what each one should get; and the tunic was left over. The tunic was without a seam, woven in one piece from top to bottom. "Let's not tear it," they said

---

* Some of our best manuscripts, including Papyrus 75, omit this first word from the cross.

to one another, "but let's throw lots and see who gets it" — what the Bible said had to come true: *They divided My clothes among them, and for My garment they threw lots.*[178] So that's what the soldiers did. Then they sat down there and kept watch over Him.

Pilate also wrote a notice, stating why Jesus was being punished, and they put it above His head on the cross. It read: THIS IS JESUS FROM NAZARETH, THE KING OF THE JEWS. Many Jews read this notice, because the place where Jesus was crucified was near the city, and it was written in Aramaic, Latin, and Greek.

Then the high priests of the Jews told Pilate, "Don't write, 'The King of the Jews,' but, 'He said, "I am the King of the Jews." ' "

Pilate answered, "What I've written I've written."

The people stood there *watching.*[179] Those who passed by were abusing Him, *shaking their heads* [180] and saying, "Ha! You tear down the temple and build it in three days — save Yourself if You are God's Son, and come down from the cross."

In the same way the ruling priests, with the Bible scholars and elders, *sneering* [179] and making fun of Him among themselves, said, "He saved others — He can't save Himself. He should save Himself if He's the Savior whom God has chosen. He's King of Israel — He should come down from the cross now. He should let us see that, and we'll believe Him. *He trusts God — God deliver Him now, seeing He delights in Him.*[181] He said, 'I am God's Son.' "

The soldiers also made fun of Him by going up to Him and *offering Him sour wine.*[177] "If You're the King of the Jews," they said, "save Yourself."

A Robber Turns to Jesus

In the same way also the robbers crucified with Him insulted Him. One of the crucified criminals was mocking Him, "Aren't You the promised Savior? Save Yourself and us!"

But the other warned him. "Aren't you afraid of God?" he asked him. "You're condemned just as He is. Our punishment is just. We're getting what we deserve for what we've done. But this One has done nothing wrong."

Then he said, "Jesus, remember me when You come to Your kingdom."

"I tell you the truth," Jesus said to him, "today you will be with Me in Paradise."

Mary

Now, His mother and her sister, Mary the wife of Clopas, and Mary from Magdala were standing near Jesus' cross.

Jesus saw His mother and the disciple He loved standing near. "Woman," He said to His mother, "there is your son!" Then He said to the disciple, "There is your mother!"

The disciple took her and from that time on had her in his home.

Three Dark Hours

It was about twelve o'clock when darkness came over the whole country, because the sun stopped shining, and the darkness lasted till three in the afternoon.

About three o'clock Jesus called out loud, *"Eloi, Eloi, lama sabachthani?"* [182] which means, "My God, My God, why did You forsake Me?"

Hearing Him, some of those standing near said, "Listen! He's calling Elijah."

After this, knowing everything had now been done, and to have the words of the Bible come true, Jesus said, *"I am thirsty."*

A jar full of *sour wine* was standing there. And immediately one of the men ran, took a sponge, soaked it in *sour wine*, put it on a hyssop stem, held it to His mouth, and *gave*

Him a drink.[177] "Let's see," he and the others said, "if Elijah comes to save Him and take Him down."

When Jesus had taken the wine, He said, *"It is finished."* [183]

Jesus Dies

But Jesus called out loud again, "Father, *into Your hands I entrust My spirit."* [184] After He said this, He bowed His head and gave up His spirit.

Just then the curtain in the temple was torn in two from top to bottom, the earth was shaken, the rocks were split, the graves were opened, and many bodies of the holy people asleep in death were brought back to life; they came out of the graves and after He had risen went into the holy city, where many saw them.

When the captain who stood facing Jesus saw how He gave up His spirit, he praised God and said, "This Man certainly was righteous." When he and those watching Jesus with him saw the earthquake and the other things happening, they were terrified. "He certainly was the Son of God!" they said.

When all the people who had come there to see this saw what happened, they beat their breasts and turned back.

All *His friends were standing at a distance,*[185] also many women who had followed Him from Galilee and had come up to Jerusalem with Him to help Him and now were watching these things. Among them were Mary from Magdala and Mary, the mother of James the Less and of Joseph, and Salome, the mother of Zebedee's sons. While He was in Galilee, they had followed Him and helped Him.

No Bone Broken

Since it was Friday and the Jews didn't want the bodies to stay on the crosses on Saturday, because that Sabbath was an important day, they asked Pilate to have the legs of the men broken and the bodies taken away. So the soldiers came and broke the legs of the first man and then of the other who had been crucified with Him.

But when they came to Jesus and saw He was dead already, they didn't break His legs, but one of the soldiers stuck a spear into His side, and immediately blood and water came out. He who saw it has testified about it, and his testimony is true, and he knows he is telling the truth so that you too will believe.

In this way what the Bible said had to come true: *None of His bones will be broken.*[186] And it says in another place, *They will look at Him whom they pierced.*[187]

Jesus Is Buried

There was a man by the name of Joseph, an important member of the Jewish court, a good and righteous man who had not voted for their plan and action. He was from Arimathea, a Jewish town, and was looking forward to God's kingdom. He had also become a disciple of Jesus, but secretly because he was afraid of the Jews.

In the evening, since it was the day of preparation, that is, Friday, Joseph dared to go to Pilate and ask him to let him take Jesus' body away.

Pilate was surprised He was already dead. He called the captain and asked him, "Has He died already?" When the captain told him, Pilate ordered the body given to Joseph.

Joseph bought some linen and came and took Jesus' body down. Then came also Nicodemus, who had first come to Jesus at night. He brought a mixture of myrrh and aloes, about seventy-two pounds. They took Jesus' body away and wrapped it with the spices in some clean linen according to the Jewish custom of burying the dead.

There was a garden at the place where Jesus was crucified, and in the garden was Joseph's own unused grave that he had cut in the rock, in which no one had yet been laid. Here, then — because it was Friday (when the Jews got ready for the Sabbath) and the day of rest was just starting and the grave was near — they laid Jesus.

The women who had come with Him from Galilee followed close behind. Mary from Magdala and the other Mary, the mother of Joses, were there. Sitting opposite the grave, they watched where and how His body was laid. After rolling a big stone against the door of the grave, Joseph went away. Then the women went back and prepared spices and perfumes. But on Saturday they rested according to the commandment.

The Guard

The next day — the Saturday after the day of preparation — the ruling priests and Pharisees met with Pilate. "Sir," they said, "we remember how that deceiver said while He was still alive, 'On the third day I will rise.' Now, order the grave to be made secure till the third day, or His disciples may come and steal Him and tell the people, 'He rose from the dead.' Then the last deception will be worse than the first."

"Take a guard," Pilate told them; "go and make it as secure as you know how."

So they went and secured the grave by sealing the stone and setting the guard.

·12·
Our Risen Savior

Jesus Rises

On Saturday evening Mary from Magdala, Mary the mother of James, and Salome bought spices to go and anoint Jesus.

Very early on Sunday morning there was a great earthquake. The Lord's angel came down from heaven, went and rolled the stone away, and sat on it. He was as bright as lightning, and his clothes were as white as snow. The guards were so afraid of him they shook and became like dead men.

While it was still dark, the women went to look at the grave. They were coming to the grave very early when the sun was up and were bringing the spices they had prepared. "Who is going to roll away the stone for us from the door of the grave?" they asked one another; it was very large. But when they looked up, they saw the stone had been rolled back.

So Mary from Magdala ran and came to Simon Peter and the other disciple, whom Jesus loved. "They've taken the Lord out of the grave," she told them, "and we don't know where they laid Him."

The other women went into the grave, but they didn't find the body of the Lord Jesus. While they were troubled about this, suddenly two men stood beside them in clothes that flashed like lightning, one young man, dressed in a white robe, sitting at the right. The women were terrified, and they bowed down to the ground.

"Don't be afraid," the angel said to the women. "I know you're looking for Jesus from Nazareth, who was crucified. Why do you look among the dead for Him who is alive? He is not here. He has risen as He said. Remember what He told you while He was still in Galilee, 'The Son of Man must be handed over to sinful men, be crucified, and rise on the third day.'" They remembered what He said. "Come, see the place where He was lying. And go quickly, tell His disciples and Peter, 'He has risen from the dead. You know, He is going ahead of you to Galilee. There you will see Him, as He told you.' Now, I have told you."

They went out and hurried away from the grave, because they were trembling and bewildered with fear and great joy. They were so frightened they didn't tell anybody anything but ran to tell His disciples.

Peter and John

So Peter and the other disciple started out for the grave. The two were running side by side, but the other disciple ran faster than Peter and got to the grave first. He looked in and saw the linen wrappings lying there but didn't go in.

When Simon Peter got there after him, he went into the grave. He bent down and saw only the linen cloths lying there, also the cloth that had been on Jesus' head, not lying with the linen wrappings but rolled up in a place by itself. Then the other disciple, who got to the grave first, also went in, saw it, and believed. They didn't know yet what the Bible meant when it said He had to rise from the dead.

So the disciples went home again, and Peter was amazed at what had happened.

"Mary!"

After Jesus rose early on Sunday, He showed Himself first to Mary from Magdala, out of whom He had driven seven devils.

Mary stood outside facing the grave and crying. As she cried, she looked into the grave and saw two angels in white clothes sitting where Jesus' body had been lying, one at the head and the other at the feet. "Woman, why are you crying?" they asked her.

"They've taken my Lord away," she told them, "and I don't know where they laid Him."

After she said this, she turned around and saw Jesus standing there but didn't know it was Jesus. "Woman, why are you crying?" Jesus asked her. "Whom are you looking for?"

"Sir," she said to Him, thinking He was the gardener, "if you carried Him away, tell me where you laid Him, and I will take Him away."

Jesus said to her, "Mary!"

She turned. "Rabboni!" she said to Him in the Jewish language. (The word means "Teacher.")

"Don't hold on to Me," Jesus told her. "I didn't go up to the Father yet. But go to My brothers and tell them, 'I am going up to My Father and your Father, to My God and your God.'"

Mary from Magdala went to those who had been with Him and were now mourning and crying and told the disciples, "I saw the Lord," and that He said this to her. When they heard He was alive and had been seen by her, they didn't believe it.

The Other Women See Jesus

The other women left the grave, went back, and there — Jesus met them and said, "Good morning!" They went up to Him, took hold of His feet, and worshiped Him.

Then Jesus said to them, "Don't be afraid. Go, tell My brothers to go to Galilee, and there they will see Me."

They reported all this to the eleven and all the others. It was Mary from Magdala, Johanna, Mary the mother of James, and the other women with them that told the apostles about it.

The apostles thought it was nonsense and wouldn't believe them.

The Guards

While the women were on their way, some of the guards went into the city and told the high priests everything that happened.

These met with the elders and agreed on a plan. They gave the soldiers a large sum of money and told them, "Say, 'His disciples came at night and stole Him while we were sleeping.' And if this comes to a hearing before the governor, we'll persuade him and see that you have nothing to worry about."

They took the money and did as they were told. And that story has been spread among the Jews to this day.

On the Way to Emmaus

Later, on the same day, two of them were walking into the country, going to a village called Emmaus, about seven miles from Jerusalem. They were talking about everything that had happened.

While they were talking and discussing, Jesus Himself joined them and walked with them. They saw Him but were kept from knowing who He was — He appeared in a different form.

"What are you discussing as you're walking along?" He asked them.

They stood still and looked gloomy. "Are you the only stranger living in Jerusalem," the one by the name of Cleopas asked Him, "who doesn't know what happened there these days?"

"What do you mean?" He asked.

"All about Jesus from Nazareth," they told Him, "who was a prophet, mighty in what He did and said before God and all the people, and how our high priests and rulers handed Him over to be condemned to death and crucified Him. But we were hoping He would be the One to free Israel. What is more, this is now the third day since it happened. And then some of our women startled us. They went to the grave early this morning and didn't find His body. They came and told us they had even seen a vision of angels who said He is alive. Some of our men went to the grave and found it as the women had said; and they didn't see Him."

"How foolish you are," He told them, "and how slow to believe everything the prophets said! Didn't the promised Savior have to suffer this and so go to His glory?" Then He explained to them, starting with Moses and all the prophets, what they said about Him in all their writings.

And so they came near the village where they were going, and He acted as if He were going farther. "Stay with us," they urged Him. "It's getting late, and the day is almost gone." So He went in to stay with them.

While He was at the table with them, He took the bread, blessed and broke it, and gave it to them. Then their eyes were opened, and they knew who He was. But He vanished from them.

"Didn't our hearts glow," they said to each other, "as He was talking to us on the way and explaining the Bible to us?"

That same hour they started out, went back to Jerusalem, and found the eleven and those who were with them all together. These said, "The Lord really did rise, and Simon saw Him."

Then the two men told the others what had happened on the way and how they had recognized Him while He was breaking the bread. But these didn't believe them.

Behind Locked Doors

That Sunday evening the doors were locked where the disciples were, because they were afraid of the Jews. He showed Himself to the eleven while they were lying at the table. While they were talking about what had happened, Jesus came and stood among them. "Peace to you!" He said to them.

They were startled and terrified and thought they were seeing a ghost.

"Why are you troubled?" He asked them. "And why do doubts come into your minds? Look at My hands and My feet: it is I Myself. Feel Me and see. A ghost doesn't have flesh and bones as you see Me have." As He said this, He showed them His hands and His feet and His side.

Then the disciples were delighted to see the Lord. They were so happy — they thought it was too good to be true — and they were surprised. "Do you have anything here to eat?" He asked them. They gave Him a piece of broiled fish. He took it and ate it while they watched Him.

Then He scolded them because their minds were closed and they didn't believe those who had seen Him after He had risen.

"While I was still with you," He said to them, "I told you that everything written about Me in the Law of Moses, the prophets, and the Psalms must come true." Then He opened their minds to understand the Bible. "This," He told them, "is what is written: The promised Savior will suffer, rise from the dead on the third day, and in His name you will preach to all people, beginning at Jerusalem, that they repent of their sins so that they will be forgiven. You will testify of these things.

"Peace to you!" Jesus said to them again. "As the Father sent Me, so I send you." When He had said this, He breathed on them and said, "Receive the Holy Spirit. If you forgive sins, they are forgiven; if you don't forgive them, they're not forgiven."

Thomas Sees Jesus

But Thomas, one of the twelve, who was called Twin, was not with them when Jesus came. So the other disciples told him, "We saw the Lord."

"Unless I see the marks of the nails in His hands," he told them, "and put my finger in the marks of the nails and put my hand in His side, I won't believe it."

A week later His disciples were again in the house, and Thomas was with them. The doors were locked, but Jesus came and stood among them. "Peace to you!" He said. Then He told Thomas, "Put your finger here, and look at My hands — and take your hand and put it in My side. And don't doubt but believe."

"My Lord and my God!" Thomas answered Him.

"Do you believe because you've seen Me?" Jesus asked him. "Blessed are those who didn't see Me and still believed."

Breakfast with Jesus

After this the eleven disciples went to Galilee, where Jesus had told them to go. There Jesus showed Himself again to the disciples at the Lake of Galilee. This is how He showed Himself.

Simon Peter, Thomas (called Twin), Nathanael from Cana in Galilee, Zebedee's sons, and two other disciples of

Jesus were together. Simon Peter said to the others, "I'm going fishing."

"We're going with you," they told him.

They went out and got into the boat. But that night they caught nothing. When morning came, Jesus stood on the shore. But the disciples didn't know it was Jesus.

"Boys, you don't have any fish, do you?" Jesus asked them.

They answered Him, "No."

"Drop the net on the right side of the boat," He told them, "and you will find some." So they dropped it. And now they couldn't pull it in, there were so many fish.

The disciple whom Jesus loved said to Peter, "It is the Lord." When Simon Peter heard him say, "It is the Lord," he put on the coat he had taken off, fastened it with his belt, and jumped into the lake. But the other disciples, who were not far from the shore, only about a hundred yards, came in the small boat, dragging the net full of fish.

As they stepped out on the shore, they saw burning coals there with fish lying on them, and bread.

"Bring some of the fish you just caught," Jesus told them. Simon Peter got into the small boat and pulled the net on the shore. It was filled with a hundred and fifty-three big fish. Although there were so many, the net wasn't torn.

"Come, have breakfast," Jesus told them. None of the disciples dared to ask Him, "Who are You?" They knew it was the Lord. Jesus came, took the bread, and gave it to them, and also the fish.

This was the third time Jesus showed Himself to the disciples after He rose from the dead.

"Do You Love Me?"

When they had eaten breakfast, Jesus asked Simon Peter "Simon, son of John, do you love Me more than these do?"

"Yes, Lord," he answered Him, "You know I love You."

"Feed My lambs," Jesus told him.

"Simon, son of John," He asked him a second time, "do you love Me?"

"Yes, Lord," he answered Him, "You know I love You."

"Be a shepherd of My sheep," Jesus told him.

"Simon, son of John," He asked him a third time, "do you love Me?"

Peter felt sad because He asked him a third time, "Do you love Me?" "Lord, You know everything," he answered Him, "You know I love You."

"Feed My sheep," Jesus told him. "I tell you the truth: When you were younger, you used to fasten your belt and go where you wanted to. But when you're old, you'll stretch out your hands, and someone else will tie you and take you where you don't want to go." He said this to show by what kind of death Peter would glorify God. After saying this, He told him, "Follow Me."

Peter turned and saw the disciple whom Jesus loved following them. He was the one who at the supper leaned against Jesus' breast and asked, "Lord, who is going to betray You?" When Peter saw him, he asked Jesus, "Lord, what about him?"

"If I want him to stay till I come," Jesus answered him, "what is that to you? You follow Me." And so it was said among the Christians, "That disciple will not die." But Jesus didn't say, "He will not die," but, "If I want him to stay till I come, what is that to you?"

This is the disciple who testified about these things and wrote this. And we know what he testifies is true.

"Go!"

The eleven disciples went to the mountain in Galilee where Jesus had told them to go. When they saw Him, they worshiped Him, but some doubted.

Coming nearer, Jesus spoke to them. "I have been given

all power in heaven and on earth," He said. "Go and make disciples of all people: Baptize them into the name of the Father, the Son, and the Holy Spirit, and teach them to do everything I have commanded you. And remember, I am with you always till the end of the world."

Jesus Goes Up to Heaven

After His suffering Jesus in many convincing ways proved to the apostles He was alive as He showed Himself to them during forty days and talked about God's kingdom.

When He met with them, He ordered them not to leave Jerusalem. "I am sending you Him whom My Father promised — you heard Me tell about Him: John baptized with water, but in a few days you will be baptized with the Holy Spirit. Wait here in the city till you are armed with power from above."

When they came together, He took them out to a place where Bethany lay ahead of them.

"Lord," they asked Him, "are You now going to make Israel an independent kingdom again?"

"It isn't for you to know," He told them, "what times or periods the Father has set by His own authority. But when the Holy Spirit comes on you, you will receive power and will testify of Me in Jerusalem, in all Judea and Samaria, and to the farthest parts of the world."

When He had said this, He raised His hands and blessed them. While He was blessing them and they were watching Him, He was lifted up, and a cloud took Him away so they couldn't see Him anymore. The Lord was *taken up to heaven and sat down at the right of God.*[188]

As He was going and they were gazing up into the sky, two men in white clothes were standing right beside them. "Men of Galilee," they asked, "why are you standing here looking up to heaven? This Jesus, who was taken away from you to heaven, will come back the same way you saw Him go to heaven."

They knelt and worshiped Jesus. Then they left the Mount of Olives, as it was called (it's near Jerusalem, only half a mile away), and went back to Jerusalem very happy. And they were always in the temple praising God.

———————

The disciples went out and preached everywhere, and the Lord worked with them and confirmed the Word by the wonderful proofs that went with it.

AMEN

His disciples saw Jesus do many other things, also many other miracles that are not written in this book. If every one of these were written, I suppose the world would not have room for the books that would be written. But these things are written so that you believe

JESUS IS THE PROMISED SAVIOR,
GOD'S SON,

and by believing have life in His name.

After May 18, A. D. 30   219

THE SON OF MAN

This is a record showing how Jesus Christ was a descendant of David and of Abraham. Jesus, who is called Christ, was the Son of Mary and, as people thought, of Mary's husband, of Joseph, of —

(Luke)	(Matthew)
Heli	Jacob
Matthat	Matthan
Levi	Eleazar
Melchi	Eliud
Jannai	Achim
Joseph	Zadok
Mattathias	Azor
Amos	Eliakim
Nahum	
Esli	
Naggai	
Maath	
Mattathias	
Semein	
Josech	
Joda	
Joanan	Abiud
Rhesa	
Zerubbabel	Zerubbabel
Shealtiel	Shealtiel
Neri	Jechoniah after the people had been taken away to Babylon. During the Babylonian Captivity Jechoniah and his brothers were the sons of
Melchi	
Addi	Josiah
Cosam	Amon
Elmadam	Manasseh
Er	Hezekiah
Jesus	Ahaz
Eliezer	Jotham
Jorim	Uzziah
Matthat	
Levi	
Simeon	
Judas	Joram
Joseph	Jehoshaphat
Jonam	Asa
Eliakim	Abijah
Melea	Rehoboam

(Luke)	(Matthew)
Menna	
Mattatha	
Nathan	Solomon, the son of Uriah's wife
David	David
Jesse	Jesse
Obed	Obed, the son of Ruth
Boaz	Boaz, the son of Rahab
Salmon	Salmon
Nahshon	Nahshon
Amminadab	Amminadab
Ram	Ram
Admin	
Arni	
Hezron	Hezron
Perez	Perez and Zerah were the sons of Tamar
Judah	Judah and his brothers
Jacob	Jacob
Isaac	Isaac
Abraham	Abraham
Terah	So there are, in all, fourteen generations from Abraham to David, fourteen from David to the Babylonian Captivity, and fourteen from the Babylonian Captivity to Christ.
Nahor	
Serug	
Reu	
Peleg	
Eber	
Shelah	
Cainan	
Arphaxad	
Shem	
Noah	
Lamech	
Methuselah	
Enoch	
Jared	
Mahalaleel	
Cainan	
Enos	
Seth	
Adam	
God	

OLD TESTAMENT REFERENCES

1. Dan. 10:12
2. Gen. 17:19
3. Num. 6:3;
   Judges 13:4
4. Mal. 4:5, 6
5. Is. 7:14
6. 2 Sam. 7:12-14, 16;
   Is. 9:7; Micah 4:7;
   1 Chron. 17:12-14
7. Gen. 18:14
8. 1 Sam. 2:1;
   Hab. 3:18
9. 1 Sam. 1:11
10. Ps. 111:9
11. Ps. 103:17
12. Ps. 89:10
13. Job 5:11; 12:19;
    Ezek. 21:26
14. Ps. 107:9
15. Is. 41:8, 9
16. Ps. 98:3
17. Gen. 17:7;
    Micah 7:20
18. Ps. 41:13; 72:18;
    89:52; 106:48
19. Ps. 111:9
20. 1 Sam. 2:10;
    Ps. 18:2; 132:17
21. Ps. 106:10
22. Micah 7:20
23. Gen. 22:16, 17;
    Lev. 26:42;
    Ps. 105:8, 9; 106:45
24. Mal. 3:1
25. Ps. 107:10; Is. 9:2
26. Is. 59:8
27. Is. 7:14; 8:8, 10
28. Lev. 12:6
29. Ex. 13:12
30. Lev. 5:11; 12:8;
    Num. 6:10
31. Is. 40:5; 52:10
32. Is. 42:6; 46:13;
    49:6
33. 2 Sam. 5:2;
    Micah 5:2, 4

34. Ps. 72:10, 15; Is. 60:6
35. Hosea 11:1
36. Jer. 31:15
37. 1 Sam. 2:26
38. Mal. 3:1
39. Is. 40:3-5
40. Ps. 2:7; Is. 42:1
41. Deut. 8:3
42. Ps. 91:11,12
43. Deut. 6:16
44. Deut. 6:13
45. Is. 40:3
46. Gen. 28:12
47. Gen. 41:55
48. Ps. 69:9
49. Is. 58:6; 61:1, 2
50. 1 Kings 17:9
51. 2 Kings 5:14
52. Is. 9:1, 2
53. Is. 53:4
54. Lev. 13:7, 49
55. Hosea 6:6
56. Lev. 24:5-8;
    1 Sam. 21:6
57. Is. 41:8, 9; 42:1-4;
    Hab. 1:4
58. Is. 57:15
59. Is. 61:2
60. Ps. 37:11
61. 2 Sam. 22:26;
    Ps. 18:25
62. Ps. 24:4
63. Ex. 20:13;
    Deut. 5:17
64. Ex. 20:14;
    Deut. 5:18
65. Deut. 24:1
66. Lev. 19:12
67. Num. 30:2;
    Deut. 23:21;
    Ps. 50:14
68. Is. 66:1
69. Ps. 48:2
70. Ex. 21:24;
    Lev. 24:20;
    Deut. 19:21

71. Lev. 19:18
72. Deut. 18:13
73. 2 Kings 4:33;
    Is. 26:20
74. Jer. 14:14; 27:15
75. Ps. 6:8
76. Mal. 1:11
77. 1 Kings 17:23
78. Is. 29:18; 35:5;
    61:1
79. Ex. 23:20;
    Mal. 3:1
80. Jonah 1:17
81. Ps. 78:2
82. Is. 6:9, 10
83. Joel 3:13
84. Ps. 104:12;
    Ezek. 17:23; 31:6;
    Dan. 4:12, 21
85. Zeph. 1:3;
    Job 12:16
86. Dan. 12:3
87. Num. 27:17;
    1 Kings 22:17;
    Ezek. 34:5
88. Micah 7:6
89. Esther 5:3; 7:2
90. Num. 27:17;
    1 Kings 22:17;
    Ezek. 34:5
91. Ex. 16:4, 15;
    Ps. 78:24
92. Is. 54:13
93. Is. 29:13
94. Ex. 20:12;
    Deut. 5:16
95. Ex. 21:17;
    Lev. 29:9
96. Jer. 5:21;
    Ezek. 12:2
97. Ps. 62:12;
    Prov. 24:12
98. Ps. 2:7; Is. 42:1;
    Deut. 18:15
99. Is. 66:24
100. Deut. 19:15

101. 2 Kings 1:10, 12
102. 2 Sam. 7:12;
     Micah 5:2
103. Ezek. 34:23
104. Is. 14:13, 15
105. Ps. 91:13
106. Jer. 6:16
107. Deut. 6:5
108. Lev. 19:18
109. Lev. 18:5
110. Micah 7:6
111. Ps. 82:6
112. Ps. 6:8
113. Mal. 1:11
114. Jer. 12:7; 22:5
115. Ps. 118:26
116. Deut. 24:1
117. Gen. 1:27; 5:2
118. Gen. 2:24
119. Lev. 13:7, 49
120. Ex. 20:12-16;
     Deut. 5:16-20
121. Lev. 19:18
122. Gen. 18:14;
     Job 42:2;
     Zech. 8:6
123. Ezek. 34:16
124. Is. 40:9; 62:11;
     Zech. 9:9
125. Ps. 118:25, 26
126. Ps. 137:9
127. Ps. 8:2
128. Is. 56:7
129. Jer. 7:11
130. Is. 5:1, 2
131. Ps. 118:22, 23

132. Gen. 38:8;
     Deut. 25:5, 6
133. Ex. 3:6
134. Deut. 6:4, 5
135. Lev. 19:18
136. Deut. 4:35; 6:4, 5
137. 1 Sam. 15:22
138. Ps. 110:1
139. Jer. 12:7; 22:5
140. Ps. 118:26
141. Ps. 6:3
142. Is. 53:1
143. Is. 6:10
144. Dan. 2:28
145. Is. 19:2;
     2 Chron. 15:6
146. Dan. 11:41
147. Micah 7:6
148. Dan. 9:27;
     11:31; 12:11
149. Deut. 32:35;
     Hosea 9:7
150. Dan. 12:1
151. Is. 63:18;
     Zech. 12:3
152. Deut. 13:1
153. Is. 13:10; 34:4
154. Ps. 65:7
155. Is. 34:4
156. Zech. 12:10, 12
157. Dan. 7:13
158. Is. 27:13
159. Deut. 30:4;
     Zech. 2:6
160. Gen. 7:6, 7
161. Gen. 19:24, 25

162. Gen. 19:17, 26
163. Is. 24:17
164. Zech. 14:5
165. Dan. 12:2
166. Zech. 11:12
167. Ps. 41:9
168. Ex. 24:8;
     Jer. 31:32;
     Zech. 9:11
169. Is. 53:12
170. Ps. 35:19;
     69:4
171. Is. 66:14
172. Zech. 13:7
173. Ps. 42:5; 43:5
174. Ps. 110:1;
     Dan. 7:13
175. Jer. 32:6-9;
     Zech. 11:12, 13
176. Hosea 10:8
177. Ps. 69:21
178. Ps. 22:18
179. Ps. 22:7
180. Ps. 109:25
181. Ps. 22:8
182. Ps. 22:1
183. Ps. 22:31
184. Ps. 31:5
185. Ps. 38:11
186. Ex. 12:46;
     Num. 9:12;
     Ps. 34:20
187. Zech. 12:10
188. Ps. 110:1;
     2 Kings 2:11

THE LIFE OF CHRIST

229

* The two oldest and best manuscripts do not have Mark 16:9-20 but end
ark's Gospel with verse 8.

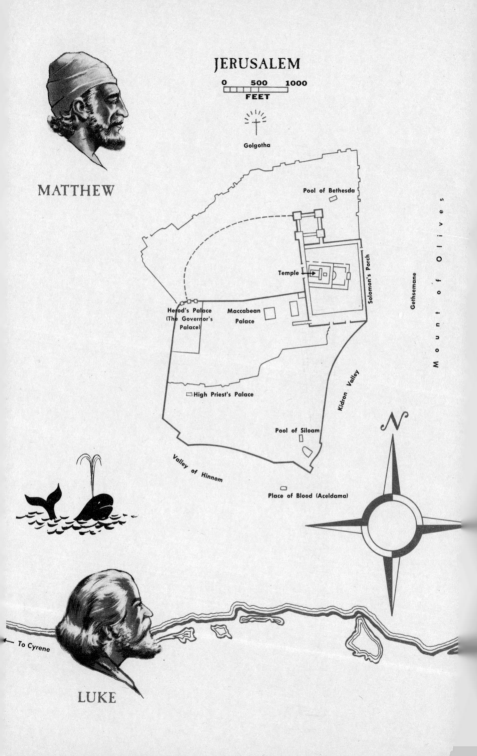

JERUSALEM

0   500   1000
FEET

Golgotha

MATTHEW

Pool of Bethesda

Temple

Solomon's Porch

Gethsemane

Mount of Olives

Herod's Palace
(The Governor's
Palace)

Maccabean
Palace

High Priest's Palace

Kidron Valley

Pool of Siloam

Valley of Hinnom

Place of Blood (Aceldama)

N

To Cyrene

LUKE